"A DIFFERENT KIND OF *Wonderful*"

"A DIFFERENT KIND OF *Wonderful*"

A Guide To Help Parents With "Special-Needs Children" Come in Out Of The Dark

∞

Tamara Jacobson
and
Lori Eichler

Assisted by: Dianne Steinberg

Copyright © 2012 by Tamara Jacobson and Lori Eichler.

Library of Congress Control Number: 2011914932
ISBN: Hardcover   978-1-4653-5559-1
                 Softcover   978-1-4653-5558-4
                 Ebook   978-1-4653-5560-7

All rights reserved. No part of this book may be reproduced or transmitted in any form or by any means, electronic or mechanical, including photocopying, recording, or by any information storage and retrieval system, without permission in writing from the copyright owner.

This book was printed in the United States of America.

To order additional copies of this book, contact:
Xlibris Corporation
1-888-795-4274
www.Xlibris.com
Orders@Xlibris.com
95972

Contents

Foreword 7

PART I   **STORIES OF US**

Chapter I   Rocky
              Near-Drowning
              (Alabama) 13

Chapter II   Ella Hears the Music
              Ataxic Cerebral Palsy (Mixed Tone),
              Aphasia, Cortical Visual Impairment
              (New Jersey) 24

Chapter III   Amazing Ryder
              Pierre Robin Syndrome/Hypotonia
              (Washington) 41

Chapter IV   Our Precious Fruit
              Cerebral Palsy / Hypotonia / Severe Athetoid CP
              (Tennessee) 55

Chapter V   Santosh the Superhero
              Autism/Hypotonia
              (Ontario, Canada) 66

Chapter VI   Marykate and Me
              Rett Syndrome
              (New Jersey) 75

Chapter VII   Wild-West Wyatt
              Spastic Quad Cerebral Palsy/ Hyper-Tonia
              (Vermont) 84

PART II EDUCATIONAL PHOTO GALLERY

PART III A COCKTAIL FOR SUCCESS

Chapter VIII The Neo Intensive Care Unit (NICU) 121

Chapter IX Conductive Education (CE) 128

Chapter X Physical Therapies: NDT, MEDEK, and SUIT THERAPY.... 135

Chapter XI Applied Behavioral Analysis (ABA) 151

Chapter XII Hyperbaric Oxygen Therapy (HBOT) 160

Chapter XIII Stem Cell Replacement Therapy 166

Chapter XIV Deal with IEP and Your School District 173

PART IV CONCLUSION

Foreword

Throughout this book are true stories provided by very special hardworking families who have children with special needs. These families are determined to help their children, however disabled, to become the most that they can be. The aim of this book is to change the landscape here in the United States, and abroad, for differently abled children. This will impact their families, their therapists, and their caregivers. If we can educate the families of these children and also those whom they interact with on a regular basis, we believe we can provide the guidance and direction these families so desperately need. We'll offer advice, hope, and a special kinship that only other special-needs families can provide. We plan to act not only as a resource, but also as providers of opinions on aggressive therapies that we have actually experienced with our own children. Just as our children are not "one size fits all," so our recommendations are also varied.

Your unexpected life journey begins the very moment that you recognize—or in some cases, are forced to admit—that your child is different from others. If the *normal* child fits between letters *A* and *H*, yours is out there somewhere in *R*. But what's supposed to happen now? Where do you turn? Right there and then, you face a million decisions. Before you're finished with this book, you'll learn to be an exceptional mom or dad, an occupational therapist, a physical therapist, a speech therapist, a teacher, a dean, a counselor, a warrior, and mostly, a fierce advocate. You'll have to stay focused, and more importantly, you'll need to be tough. You'll be constantly learning something new, whether you like it or not. What's a neonatologist, developmental pediatrician, neurologist, physiatrist, gastroenterologist, allergist, and pulmonologist? You will learn about specialists, such as special-needs dentists, for instance. What's special about a children's hospital? What does *early intervention* mean to your child and your family? We will be addressing all these questions and more.

How much will all this cost you, both financially and emotionally? How is this child going to fit into the lives of your other family members such as siblings, grandparents, aunts, uncles, and friends? How much or little support will you receive from your local and greater community as well as from the state and federal government? Will you have to give up family trips or one or two extracurricular activities for your other children now that this child needs so much more attention? What else must you neglect because of the concerns of a special-needs child, and what new concerns must be addressed?

We hope that as we share our personal journeys with you, you'll get important information that will reduce your distress, alleviate your fears, and help you solve problems. We will provide answers to your questions, send you off in the right direction, and offer you comfort.

The parents interviewed in this book desire only to share their hard-won truths and discoveries. They hope to make you an informed parent or guardian right at the beginning of your quest, before confusion clouds your judgment and differing diagnosis lead you astray.

Life is a journey, and journeys always have guides: handbooks, maps, personal anecdotes and ratings, unexpected twists and turns, and opportunities for profound growth. Although no one can provide you with a detailed map, we can offer you the wisdom we've acquired. Hopefully, that will guide you on the necessary route that you and your family need to take. So take it slow and try not to feel totally overwhelmed. We've all been there, and here's what we discovered: you *can* be assertive and strong, and you *can* make wise decisions as you investigate all your options. We've done it, and we know that you *can* do it too!

When you come directly out of the hospital or therapy center with your beautiful new arrival, you are absolutely entitled to receive early intervention services to meet you and your baby at your home. Early intervention begins at *birth*. This is an important fact most people are not aware of. Parents of typical children believe early intervention begins at around two and a half years old. They believe that when or if a child walks late or talks late, they should then call the Early Intervention Office to come evaluate their child. Unfortunately, in many, many cases they have wasted valuable years of good therapy! Don't make that mistake. Have the call into your Early Intervention Office or local Board of Education Office to notify them of who you and your baby are. Do this while your baby is still in the NICU or the very minute you believe your child isn't developing typically.

Nobody usually sees himself—or herself—having to deal with these unexpected circumstances. Why would you? It's not something you ever expected or talked about. And it isn't easy! But you don't want to look back five years from now and say "I could have" or "I should have." It's too late for the many advantages of *early intervention* once your child is older. But you'll never hear anyone say, "I'm so sorry I did so much for my child." Many of us have given up a career in order to work with our children at home. Yet you'll never hear any of us say, "I'm sorry I didn't work all those years."

Another thing we've learned: make the computer your best friend. With it, you can make connections with support groups, keep up with the latest research, and learn specific symptoms and treatments. It's amazing how supportive social networking can be.

When we become parents, we have no idea what to expect. That's true for the birth of any child. So how much worse would it be when you discover that you have a child who has, and will have, a lifelong problem? To put it bluntly, any normal person would be *freakin' terrified*! What will such a calamity mean to your life? What intervention might help *even the odds* for your special child? You're sure of only one thing: you've been presented with a child who has unique problems. Perhaps you wish that someone would magically appear and say, "Listen, here's the deal . . ."

Well, guess what? Here's the deal! One day, you'll be able to look at the whole experience and say, "My child is just a *different* kind of wonderful."

All of us including Courtney with her son Denton.

Part I

Stories of Us

Chapter 1

Rocky
Near-Drowning
(Alabama)

Cole as Superman

My name is Tiffany Hicks. I have a wonderful husband named Robert and three beautiful children: Austin, aged fourteen; Briana, aged ten; and Cole, aged five. They are everything I've ever wanted in life—a perfect marriage and three healthy children.

On March 8, 2007, my world completely changed. My son Cole, who was twenty months old at the time, was discovered floating in a day care swimming pool—*lifeless*! I received the devastating phone call around ten that morning, while I was at work. A friend of mine called to tell me that I better get to the day care center because she heard that they found two babies floating in the swimming pool, but she had no idea of the identity of the children. Instantly, out of a mother's instinct, I knew it was Cole.

I was hysterical when I phoned my husband at work, and he went to the day care center since he was closer. I will never, as long as I live, forget the feeling that I had at that very moment. I felt like I was suffocating—as if someone was squeezing the life out of me. Some coworkers drove me to a church about a mile from the center, where a South Flight helicopter would be landing. I jumped out of the car and ran up to my husband, and he grabbed me and said, "Tiffany, it was Cole. Our baby is gone."

I began screaming, "*No, no, no!* He's not gone! Get out there and put him on that helicopter!"

The police officer who pulled Cole out of the water looked straight at me with tears in his eyes and said, "You need to drive to the local hospital and identify your son."

I remember saying, "Identify him? No! The helicopter is here to pick him up. Get him on it now!"

"Mr. and Mrs. Hicks, the helicopter will be taking the other child found in the pool. That child has a heartbeat," the officer explained.

So a friend of ours drove us to the local hospital. As my husband and I were stepping into the ER, a nurse ran up to us and said, "They put Cole on the helicopter. Get to Mobile now!"

We later learned that the day care owner found the other baby in the water, pulled the baby out, and started CPR. He also called 911. A state trooper arrived and took over CPR on the toddler and got a heartbeat on him. A few minutes later, another local officer pulled up and screamed, "There's another baby in the water!" He jumped in and pulled Cole out. They'd been so busy with that other baby that they didn't even notice my baby boy in the water. So Cole suffered severe brain damage, while the other toddler was fine.

Upon arriving at Women's and Children's Hospital, which is about an hour from where our small town of Jackson is located, a social worker ran up to us as we were trying to find the ER and said, "I'll take you to Cole, but you must understand, he is very, very critical!"

I kept asking her, "Is he alive? Please tell me he's alive!" She never answered. I don't think she knew the answer at that time.

When we made it to the ER, they were working very hard to keep Cole alive. His eyes were fixed, completely dilated and glazed over. He was cold to the touch. The ER doctor pulled me to the side and said, "We got a full heartbeat on him about eight minutes after he came in, but Cole is very critical."

I will never forget the words that came from her mouth after that. "Mrs. Hicks, looking Cole over and seeing his eyes being dilated as they are, you are probably looking at severe brain damage. I'm not even sure that he'll pull through," the doctor said.

My chest tightened, and every muscle on my body felt numb. I looked over at Cole and said, "Get up, baby. Mommy is here to get you!"

I just wanted to wake up from this nightmare; this couldn't be happening to me. My husband was on his knees beside Cole, saying, "Come on, buddy, pull through this for Daddy. You can do it."

After about two hours in the ER, with Cole fighting for his life, they finally got his body temperature up and his heartbeat stable enough that he could be transferred to the ICU (Intensive Critical Care Unit). Again, the doctor up there told us that Cole was a very sick little boy, and that his chances of pulling through the night were very slim. Robert and I stayed up all night, crying and praying and pleading with God to save our child. Cole did pull through the night, but little did we know that we had a very long road ahead of us.

Over the next few days, Cole was showing a little improvement. His lungs were becoming clear, and his vital signs were getting better. So on the ninth day in the hospital, they pulled Cole's breathing tube out to see if he could breathe on his own. He was doing very well on his own at first, but a little while later, you could tell it had become a struggle for him. A couple of hours later, his airway obstructed, and they had to quickly put the breathing tube back in.

After that, Cole became unresponsive and had no reflexes. The doctor told us that he was now brain dead. His MRI showed his brain shrinking, deteriorating, and pulling away from his skull—which is what happens in brain death. My husband asked, "Well, what does *brain dead* mean?"

The doctor responded, saying, "Cole is no longer with us." Again, we were in complete shock!

The nurse came in and said, "I know this is a very difficult time for your family, but we need to know if you would like to consider donating Cole's organs." After we talked for a few minutes, we decided that we would donate Cole's organs in hopes that it would help another child in need.

Quickly the nurses began putting ice packs on Cole to preserve his organs and a solution in his eyes so they would not dry out. All I could do was stand there and stare at my innocent baby, who had been given to me for such a short time. How do you say good-bye to one of the three most precious things that has graced your life?

"I would go ahead and pull the plug," said the doctor, "to make it not so hard on your family." My husband replied that since there was a twelve-hour protocol, we should let it be so and do it in the morning. A friend brought our son Austin, who was eleven at the time, and Briana, who was six, down to the hospital to see their little brother before we pulled him off life support. My son Austin was having a really hard time telling his brother good-bye, so my husband took him down to the chapel to pray and ask God to give him his little brother back. I stayed in the room with Cole the whole time. He was starting to turn blue around his lips and under his eyes, and he was very pale. The doctors told me that your brain does not make your heart beat, but that Cole's heart would stop at any time, since his brain was no longer working anything else in his body. I sat there with a stethoscope to Cole's heart, waiting to hear his last heartbeat.

After five hours of everyone traipsing in and out to say good-bye, and with Austin and Robert still in the chapel, I was sure I saw Cole twitch his nose a little bit. I hollered for the doctor and told her what I had seen, and she told me that I only thought I saw him move because I so wanted him to. He hadn't really moved, she insisted, because he was gone. Maybe I do just want to see it, I thought. Maybe I am going crazy! I really thought I was. But just as that thought was going through my mind, Cole moved his fingers and the doctor's jaw *dropped*.

Immediately, the nurse and doctor started tossing ice bags off Cole and putting towels around him to get him warm. The doctor said, "I don't know what to say, Mrs. Hicks. I've never seen anything like this before!" Later, I learned that she actually had to have counseling after this.

I truly believe that my son's prayer for his little brother's life was heard that day. If only we all had the faith of a child! Cole was alive again, in full living color. If we had done what the doctors had said and pulled the plug, Cole would not be here today.

Another few days went by, and the doctor told us that Cole would need a tracheotomy before we take the breathing tube out again. My husband looked at me once again and said, "God has had his hand in this the whole time. Let's just tell them not to put a trac in, and let God's will be done. The doctors warned us that Cole would be unable to hold his airway open again without that trac, and that he would die when we pull the breathing tube out. Once again, our whole family and our pastor came down to say their farewells to Cole. So now, this was our third time telling our little boy good-bye.

The doctor told us again that Cole's brain was so damaged that death would be the most compassionate thing one could wish for the child. All family members left the room, and Cole's breathing tube was pulled out. Robert and I took turns holding Cole and loving him and telling him how much we loved him. Over the next couple of hours, his oxygen began to drop—90 . . . 80 . . . 70 . . . 63 . . The nurse said, "It won't be long." I truly believe Cole could hear everything we were saying, because as soon as she said that, his oxygen started going back up—70 . . . 80 . . . 90 . . All Cole's stats were better now than they were before we pulled the tube out. The doctor said, "This kid is a *miracle*! He's just amazed me!"

After several days of Cole breathing on his own and all his numbers looking great, we were finally able to graduate to a regular hospital room. Then Cole was sent to a rehabilitation hospital in Birmingham, Alabama. The hospital was great. Cole was taken to therapy every day, and we did notice that he was becoming a little more alert, but not by much. Cole was still drooling and unable to swallow, so we had a feeding tube put in to support his nutritional needs. His body remained very stiff (called posturing) since he was unable to control any of his muscles. The doctor looked at us and said, "I have seen a lot of miracles in my time, and I do believe anything is possible. But remember, Cole has the worst possible injury any human being could have. Take him home and love him, because I'm not sure what his future holds."

I was thinking, okay, he's beaten all odds already. This is all going to be all right! My baby will improve every day and then be up and walking before we know it. This is how uneducated we were about the words *brain injury*. It does *not* get better within a year; it takes years of hard, dedicated work and proper therapies for your child to reach his/her highest potential. All the doctors do is give you the worst possible case scenario and send you home, with no type of plan whatsoever.

We finally made it home after a total of forty-one days in the hospital. Our family, friends, and community welcomed us home with open arms. Everyone was so happy to see Cole come home. A huge sign in our front yard read, "Welcome Home Cole." The local paper put Cole's picture on the front page with the police officer who had administered CPR on him at the day care center. It was one of the happiest days of my life. Robert looked at me and said, "Instead of planning his funeral, we have our baby at home again. God is great!"

This is the day Cole took on the name Rocky. As a hard-fighting little boy who had beaten the word *death* three times, what better name could he have? After a couple of weeks, I had to return to work, and my husband was able to stay at home with Cole. Without the outpouring of support from our family, friends, and community, we would have lost everything we owned. Robert took Cole to therapy three times a week for several months. Cole slowly made small improvements. But after two years of traditional therapies—physical therapy, occupational therapy, and speech therapy—twice a week, Cole was not making the huge improvements as I had expected.

I let myself sink into another depression. All I could think about was that it had been two years. Why was it taking so long for Cole to get better? On top of everything, Robert and I were not spending any time together, and our marriage was falling apart. Everything we did seem to revolve around Cole. Eventually, the big D word came up—*divorce*! A few months went by, and it seemed nothing was getting any better. He'd move out, then move back in, with Cole not improving as we thought he should. Finally, one day, we sat down and agreed that we had to pull through this together.

During the two years that Robert stayed at home with Cole, he worked very hard with him. He would massage every muscle and do rounds and rounds of range of motion while Cole was unable to move himself. He made four trips to Mobile a week, which is a two-hour round-trip drive every day to do physical therapy. Cole was so stiff that he could not even put him in a car seat, so he had no choice but to lay him down in the backseat of the truck with blankets all around him. Thank God, Robert never was pulled over.

All in all, you do what you have to do for your child! After about two months of being home, we started lowering the doses on all of Cole's medications. I have to say that this was a very tough time. Do you want to keep him drugged up where he can't do anything, or do you slowly wean him off with withdrawals and give him a chance? We chose to give him a chance. Slowly, we started seeing him smile. He began to follow objects with his eyes and move his arms. Within six months, Cole was off every single medication that was prescribed: Baclofen, Zanaflex, Adivan, etc.! Before we knew it, a year had passed by, and Cole had made a lot of progress—*slowly*! He began to roll and started putting his hands to his mouth. We were so happy he was moving that we just let him put his hands in his mouth, which he still has the habit until today. We're working very hard at that.

We began discussing hyperbaric oxygen therapy and decided to take Cole to a facility that had a low-pressure chamber to put him in. Robert took Cole to this facility two days a week to receive his hyperbaric treatments, and we started noticing more progress with Cole. We decided to purchase a low-pressure chamber to keep at home. Robert dropped his therapies in Mobile and started working with him more at home, doing the low-pressure oxygen treatments at home for one hour, twice a day. Robert also purchased an adaptive bike to put Cole on every afternoon. It was not very long before we decided to find a high-pressure chamber, which led us to the Ability Camp in Canada. He had made so much progress with the low-pressure chamber that we knew he could handle the high-pressure one. There, we discovered *aggressive therapy*.

The decision was made that Robert would go back to work, while I would now stay home with Cole. By the grace of God, our commitment to each other, and our devotion to our family and to Cole, our marriage started to improve. You see, when you go through a crisis like this, you have to keep your relationship strong and make sure you are spending the time together that you need. Even though you want every minute dedicated to getting your child better, you have to sometimes just set everything else aside and spend good quality time together.

Now that I had time, I immediately began surfing the Internet. I knew there had to be something more out there. The key word is *search*. No one is going to volunteer this information. You have to be the dedicated parent that is willing to go above and beyond for your child! I finally came across a listing for the Ability Camp located in Canada and became very interested in taking Cole there. I talked to Cole's doctor about it, but he told me I would just be wasting my time. I felt deep in my heart that Cole could do much more, so I just took the chance.

Cole spent five weeks in Canada doing conductive education and hyperbaric treatments. At the camp, he became verbal and started to eat by mouth. He was able to bear a little weight on his legs and became more attentive to other people and to his surroundings. We made a second five-week trip back to the camp and saw even more improvement. As a matter of fact, we saw more improvement in those ten weeks than we had seen in three years. Everyone was amazed at Cole's progress.

While we were at the Ability Camp, we met a lot of new families from all over. The camp has just a few children or adults at any given time, so the caregivers or parents get to know each other well and share their stories. It was actually a little overwhelming to learn of all the different therapies that were available to children with disabilities. People had tried using these different therapies with varying results. It was like I'd stepped into a completely different world. I was introduced to the therapy called Medek. Cole did only two weeks of Medek in New Jersey and became able to bear *all* the weight on his legs and improved greatly in his trunk strength. Apparently, Medek was the therapy he needed. We now do the exercises at home with him every day, and he's improving by leaps and bounds. We are also looking into stem cell therapy and have decided to go back for another round of hyperbaric oxygen and Medek therapies in the near future.

If I had to give any advice at all, it would be to go with your maternal instinct. Look at all the therapies available, but also look beyond the more traditional therapies. Don't let anyone fool you. There is so much out there that wasn't there fifty years ago, twenty years ago—even five years ago. It takes more than just the tried and true to get your child better.

When I think about Cole, I am optimistic about the future. But I wonder also about the past, about when I was a girl. My mother gave me advice about how to wear my clothes, how to deal with dating and periods, how to keep myself clean, but never did she prepare me for the all-important negatives. How do you handle a crisis in your marriage? What if the children are *not* all right? What if the day comes when you find you're not *sitting on top of the world?*

I had everything I wanted only to lose it in a minute. I made a lot of mistakes, partly because I wasn't prepared and partly because one really can't be prepared for what happened to Cole or to all the other children I met in Ability Camp. But these are not throwaway children. Every child with special needs has a family—and a story. What we want for these children—what I want for Cole—is the end of a fairy tale. It may not be the same as it is for a child who has no special needs, but for our children, we too want "And they lived happily ever after."

Cole and Mom

Ryder and Cole

Cole's 5th Birthday Party with his Family

Sister Briana, Brother Austin and Mom

Chapter II

Ella Hears the Music
*Ataxic Cerebral Palsy (Mixed Tone),
Aphasia, Cortical Visual Impairment*
(New Jersey)

Living friendships at "Ability Camp" in Picton, Ontario

I was on my way to my gynecological exam. I remember thinking, Wow! Another baby! Sitting there in my doctor's office, I felt my heart racing with excitement. I knew I was pregnant; I tested positive on three different home pregnancy tests. There would soon be a sister or a brother for my sweet baby Laura, who was a year and a half old. At thirty-five, I couldn't wait to grow my little family! Having kids two years apart was perfect for our family plan. I thought to myself, would it be a boy or a girl? If it were a boy, how would I take care of him? Although I have four nephews, I was a *girl* mom. Pink ribbons and braids and ballet were what I knew and loved.

My doctor did a sonogram, and my exam went well. All was fine and on schedule. At twelve weeks, I went back to the doctors for the second time. I was on the table looking at the sonogram machine. My doctor slowly turned the machine around and showed me the screen. What it revealed was shocking—I wasn't having one baby, I was having two! Oh my god, *twins*.

I was so excited. After my first daughter, Laura, I never thought I could have another child. Laura was conceived with the help of artificial insemination or IUI. I had a blocked fallopian tube and other issues, so it took a while and I needed lots of help. After Laura was born, however, I underwent laparoscopic surgery and a D&C. *Boom!* I was pregnant again. *Boom!* One egg split into two, and I was carrying twins! Identical twins!

The doctor informed me that identical twins could only happen naturally and not with IUI. I hadn't known that identical twins ran on one side of my family because we lost touch with that group of relatives. Surprise, surprise! I asked the doctor how I could tell my husband that the twins would be identical, not fraternal. She laughed and suggested that I try handing my husband a pack of Doublemint gum. She also suggested that I concentrate on the positives of two at once—one less birthday party and built-in best friends! How adorable! And we could finish our ideal family of three children with one less pregnancy. Sure, it would be harder at first, but it would get easier as the years pass.

Then came the bad news. The doctor also told me that identical twins pose an increased risk of mild-to-serious problems. We needed to see a team of high-risk doctors who would monitor me more closely than if I was carrying a single baby. She explained that both of the babies would be nurtured by a single placenta, but that there would be a thin membrane between the two. Until that moment, I had no idea that the prospect of having identical twins increased the likelihood of giving birth to a child with special needs. There is this understanding among doctors that a certain number of all multiples will be learning-disabled or much worse. Most parents don't know much about this. They think it's so cool. Twins, triplets, yay!

Since then, I've done a lot of research. I've learned that there's a 17-35 percent increased risk of disabilities with multiple births. In time, I also learned that my identical twins would have an even greater probability of problems, ranging from learning disabilities to autism to cerebral palsy. Because identical twins share that single placenta, there is always the increased risk that one could receive too little oxygen and food, while the other could be poisoned by too much. This condition is called twin-to-twin transfusion (TTS). Ever heard of it? Well, neither had I!

At the OB/high-risk doctors, I had a double amino, and everything came back great. We were so relieved! The twins were now identified as Baby A and Baby B, and they were girls. Life was good. Pink ribbons, dolls, and ballet—just as I wished. My little daughter Laura was so excited she would dress up twin dolls and stroll them around the house and give them cute names like Girl-Girl and Sally.

I had to visit the high-risk OB every month in the beginning, then every three weeks or so later. Everything was great, great, great! Then, at twenty-nine weeks, *bang!* There was a change. Baby B wasn't doing so well in passing the stress tests. I'm thinking: is it a test where she just won't be a good athlete when she grows up? To be safe, they hospitalized me and gave me steroids so that the lungs of both babies would develop faster. That way, if the babies were born early, they would be mature enough to do well.

They also told me I had a depleted amount of water in the sac and that I should drink, drink, drink. Baby B, the one showing signs of stress, would now do fine they said, and I was sent home. I remember sitting on the couch at home, with my husband pouring pitchers of so much water into me I thought I was a fish. The doctors continued monitoring. I was told to take more fluids and get more bed rest. No problem. I drank and drank and rested as much as you can when you weigh ninety extra pounds and don't see your feet and have horrible calf cramps. I felt and looked like a beached whale. I also had my adorable little Laura running circles around my bed. The doctors kept saying to keep going with bed rest. So I kept going.

At thirty-four weeks, I told them I hadn't been feeling movement from Baby B, who had locked herself in under my rib cage. The rest of the team was considering sending me home again, but I went into labor during my office visit. We demanded to see our primary physician along with the rest of the high risk team. I believe God interceded that day, because as we went downstairs to call the family, we ran into my OB. Thank God! I explained the situation and begged, "Please, doc, I'm so worried about Baby B. Will you be delivering me today or just keeping me in the hospital due to labor?" I really wanted to take the babies out immediately even though it was early, and they could have just stopped the labor. I cried to my doctor, "Aren't they big enough now to take them out?"

My primary OB said, "Absolutely! Let's do it. It's time."

The NICU team was called and was waiting for us in the delivery room. Finally, the moment we were anticipating. Baby A (Alexandra Rose), who we call Lexi, came out problem-free as promised. A few minutes later, Baby B (Elizabeth Catherine), who we call Ella, was born. We heard a high-pitched wail.

Alan, my courageous husband, was watching. He was holding my hand and telling me what was happening. The doctor told us that each baby could breathe on her own. Phew! Each of the babies was about four pounds, nine ounces—a good size for twins. But Alan noticed that Baby B was slightly blue, and the bottom right side of her lip was drooping. Something looked a little off. Later, I thought maybe she had suffered a mini stroke. Ella also had low water in her sac and had meconium staining, which we learned indicated distress.

At first, the hospital didn't mention anything other than what they had to. Twin A (Lexi) was fine, but Twin B (Ella) was born without the impulse to suck or even to swallow. Not one of her reflexes was strong. She could not nurse or take a bottle. She had a borderline high bilirubin issue, which measures jaundice in a newborn. Ella was borderline to go under the lights. We thought they should have placed her there, but they didn't share our opinion, and we weren't doctors. Many babies exhibit jaundice, but a small percentage of these children will turn out to have cerebral palsy or traumatic brain disorder. It can be a real indicator of things to come.

Meanwhile, we learned that the inability to suck or swallow is called aphasia. This is a problem emanating from the oral area such as an inability to suck, swallow, chew, or speak. A proportion of children with this condition will have the problem resolve itself in a short time in the NICU. However, Ella showed no sign of improving. Ella's case of aphasia was a crucial warning of things being very wrong. I don't want to be an alarmist, but most families I know that have a special-needs child truly had their share of aphasia or dysphasia or just major feeding issues at birth, for months, and even years afterward.

We were concerned, so we brought in a highly recommended pediatric neurologist, who did a CAT scan and found that her lacking the ability to swallow was just the tip of the iceberg. Our neurologist was reassuring, stating that at this time he didn't see typical PVL (periventricular leukomalacia) or any massive brain hemorrhage. The doctors still ordered therapy for Ella. A hospital OT (occupational therapist), Colleen, was sent in. She was really terrific. After some routine tests, she informed us that Ella's body tone (muscular development) was mixed. In other words, her body tone was too relaxed (hypotonia) to support her in some places and too tight (hypertonia) to move flexibly in others. Five years later, Colleen is still our OT and has now become *part of the family*.

A speech therapist was also assigned in the NICU. Dana was like an angel to us. An NG tube (nasogastric tube) had been inserted into Ella's nose and into her stomach to help her receive food. I was told the NG tube, which goes down through your nose, is painful and not good to use for more than a few weeks. Dana felt—along with our terrific neurologist Abba Cargan of Mountainside, New Jersey—that the NG tube was going to be intrusive and would actually prevent Ella from learning how to suck and swallow. But Ella needed something. She was surgically fitted with a G-tube (gastrostomy), a plastic tube that delivers food directly into the stomach through the belly. We were so scared to pull the NG tube and do the G-tube surgery on our two-week-old daughter. Dana felt this procedure would make her job easier. She not only had Ella in the hospital, but followed us into our home as our speech therapist! She'll always be important to us. A good therapist is worth his or her weight in gold. *Treat your therapists well!*

I kept wondering what would have happened if Ella was born fifty years ago. I know she probably would have just died. I do want to remind everyone going through this how lucky we are that a child who can't suck or swallow can be G-tube-fed. Eventually, most of them do learn how to drink and can get off the tube.

We discovered that on top of all the other stuff, she also suffered from severe GERD (gastroesophageal reflux disease), which is essentially an inability to correctly digest food. With reflux, as it is commonly known, whatever is eaten can come back up again through the esophagus. In Ella's case, taking nourishment resulted in projectile vomiting—across the room! It was really awful. You know, to this day, when people ask whether Ella has ever spit up or thrown up, I laugh as I picture milk bombs shot across the kitchen! Ella still has mild reflex, but now, when people say "Ella has some spit-up," I am like, "What are you talking about? This is nothing."

GERD caused her to lose much of what she took in. With constant testing and her loss of weight and nourishment, she had to remain at the hospital for well over a month. Then, after her long stay, the hospital wanted us to just ship her off to a specialized children's hospital, a rehab center for little people. They never explained to us how serious her condition was or why they felt she needed more attention. I was so busy with Ella that I hardly got to know or bonded with my healthy little twin, Lexi. To this day, I cry over the time I never got with my incredible, adorable little Lexi. We have a good relationship, but she feels she never gets Mommy enough. It killed me to think that a nanny was taking care of my baby and not me. Big sister Laura started at a full-day nursery school program at the age of two because I had no choice. What could I do? I had this baby who started out life as a sack of potatoes but who looked to me for life.

Looking back at our hospital experience, it was probably one of the best things that happened to us. We really did despise the facility (inevitable, I guess), but we learned how important it was to do intensive bursts of therapy even for a baby—a baby who would later be diagnosed with severe cerebral palsy. Every day, when we arrived at the hospital, we always found

Ella hysterically crying. The nurses told us that she hardly ever stopped. Was it the GERD? Was it some undiagnosed issue?

We played music for Ella, hoping to calm her. We tried different types: the Indigo Girls, James Taylor, John Denver, Barry Manilow, show tunes and classical music for nearly twenty-four hours a day. Nothing helped. To complicate matters even further, we soon discovered that, unlike other babies, Ella took no comfort from being held. In fact, she arched her back as though to avoid physical contact with any and all human beings. Perhaps, you imagine not being able to soothe your own baby. You can't take away their pain. I felt kicked in the stomach over and over again.

We decided that she could scream in our own house just as well as she could in the hospital, so at nearly five months old, Ella came home. Finally, she would reunite with her sisters, Laura and Lexi. Maybe we could start to be a real family! Not only would we have all our girls together under the same roof, but I'd also be able to give my two-and-a-half-year-old Laura and five-month-old Lexi some of the attention they so deserved. This was the beginning of my learning how to juggle the needs of my girls all living together. It's tough when a baby comes home with serious problems.

Shortly before she came home, I learned from Social Services that we were entitled to twenty-four-hour nursing care as long as extensive notes were submitted to the State. Soon after we arrived, an Early Intervention case worker visited us. Most states in the USA offer Early Intervention services, but you need to tell them you're out there. No one's going to search for you. The case worker sent us health-care professionals who knew how to hook up and use a G-tube—at first round-the-clock, then overnight only, and finally, not at all.

I also took Ella to visit a gastroenterologist to check her stomach. He agreed about the Prevacid that had been prescribed to her at the children's hospital.

Now, we learned all about finances. We had to figure out what was available through local funding, from the state, and from the federal government. This varies from location to location, but believe me, it's never as much as you need. You'll have to prioritize. Should you pay for a private therapist if the one offered by Early Intervention is no doing enough? (Obviously, you can't do this if you simply can't afford it). But it isn't only the money. It's also the allocation of time. Early Intervention is a must for babies. There just aren't enough hours in the day to take care of all the therapies that would help your child maximize his/her chance of a more *normal* life.

We took Ella to a pediatric ENT (ears/nose/throat specialist). When the doctor first saw Ella, he thought her vocal cords might be paralyzed. She did not attempt to speak and could not move her tongue or open her mouth. Later, we came to understand that her chords weren't actually paralyzed but that she had no oral control.

Our speech therapist told us about the electronic stimulation machine VitalStim that was being used on stroke victims with great success. We learned that we could use this machine for six to eight weeks for forty-five minutes a day. This was supposed to get her to swallow and to allow the vocal chords to resonate. A barium swallow study verified that each of her swallows involved a full minute of time. In other words, there was a minute of disconnect between liquid entering her mouth, being pushed to the back of her throat, and then being swallowed. You can imagine how long it would take to get enough liquid into her—several times a day! Sometimes, the liquid even went out her nose. Boy, oh boy! You'd just have to laugh, because otherwise, you'd cry!

My husband, Alan, and I still disagree about the effectiveness of VitalStim treatment. All I know is that after the use of VitalStim, Ella was able to swallow within thirty to forty seconds instead of a full minute. Alan thinks this increase in efficiently swallowing would have happened anyway with ongoing speech therapy. I think the VitalStim therapy quickened the pace. The downside is that this treatment is very expensive—approximately $4,000 for three weeks of therapy.

Another thing that helped Ella to develop a swallow was an *intensive feeding clinic* at a local hospital. I heard about the clinic from our pediatric neurologist. In our case, Ella attended two three-week sessions, which are almost a year apart, and one that specialized in feeding as well as swallowing. She hated the clinic, but it changed her life. The earlier you do it, the better. They even take babies. Ella worked very hard to learn to open her mouth and swallow. They used well-established behavioral techniques. For example, after she did something right, they would let her have an instant reward: time with a toy, a favorite song, etc. As a result, Ella improved her sip-to-swallow time still more to about fifteen seconds.

A month before her third birthday, Ella's G-tube was removed! Now at five, she has several spoken words, (We've been told not to expect too much in the way of speech), and her tongue is beginning to move laterally. She is also developing the ability to munch, although she still cannot chew and continues to eat pureed foods. She has gone from thickened drinks to drinking regular juice. However, she still uses special cut-out cups or two-handled covered sippy cups. She also has to wear glasses, but so far, her auditory skills appear to be okay.

Ella could not *find her center*. It was pitiful to watch her because she would shake her head constantly as though looking for a way to be at peace with herself. That was the first thing the therapists wanted to help her overcome. She couldn't sit up until she was eighteen months old, and she could not maintain a seat for more than a second or two. For mobility, she moved across the floor, rolling and rolling all over. We got her one of those play tunnels, and a few months later, she was able to roll/crawl/slide through. The whole family cheered!

Crawling was the next step when she was almost three. For months, she could not hold herself up. She'd maneuver onto her knees and then topple over. First, it was one step. Then two. It took almost a year for her to be able to sustain herself and then actually move. Walking was step three, and because her legs were the least impacted upon by her CP, she seemed to know what to do but couldn't hold herself up to do it. It took nearly two years, but now she does a zombie walk—without a walker!

This year, we had a wonderful three-way birthday party in a big movie theater. Laura, Lexi, and Ella were all able to celebrate their birthdays together and really enjoyed the movie party with their friends. Pink ribbons and maybe not ballet for all my girls yet, but we just signed Ella up for her first soccer team on Saturdays. Now I can watch with pride as my oldest daughter Laura, who is a fabulous figure skater, skates circles around me. I watch Ella's twin Lexi, really like my middle child, dance like a swan, and sing away. What a fantastic gymnast she is. They make me giggle all the time. And I watch as Ella kicks a ball across the living room in adaptive soccer. Now at five, I can say Ella is a real little girl.

Our neurologist's original diagnosis was that Ella had a *global delay*, but that she would continue to develop slowly, especially with therapy, and would eventually mature. He felt that we had a long road ahead of us but was optimistic, so we were too. Other doctors insisted that it was cerebral palsy, although they didn't agree on the type of CP it was. One doctor may not have all the answers, so you need to get more than one opinion. In our case, it didn't matter, since the suggested therapies were exactly the same no matter what name was applied to the condition she suffers from. For other disabilities, however, it might really matter a lot.

Now, Ella receives fifteen hours of supplemental services and attends ten hours a week at a special education handicapped pre-school within our school district. If your child has limited mobility but is capable of learning, I highly recommend you find a school like PG Chambers School for Special Needs, located in Cedar Knolls, New Jersey. It's a wonderful place with great teachers and therapists. Ella attended its program for one and a half years.

To date, Ella is currently walking independently for short distances. She walks on grass and sand and some slopes but doesn't feel really secure and wants to hold someone's hand. She still can't maneuver stairs or walk for long distances.

Chewing would be a huge accomplishment, and we haven't given up on it.

She reads about twenty sight words, babbles, and can say eight words or so. We are using the My Baby Can Read program along with the Dr. Doman program of flashcards and nursery rhymes, with children completing the words and listening to a prime parent's voice telling stories, singing, and saying the rhythms.

Our road has been long and hard, but life has such sweet rewards as well. We have had great support from our friends, our awesome extended community, and our family. We are very proud of Ella and her therapy teams in and around the world. Now, when we play music like John Denver or Barry Manilow for Ella, she sways her body and dances. We can say with full confidence that Ella hears the music!

Dad and Ella learning about "potty-training" at PG Chambers

Lexi, age 2; Laura, age 4 and Ella age 2. Family is everything!

Ella did the flew on the Trapeze!

Ella is a happy, healthy girl!

Ella on Halloween 2011

Ella's Mom and Dad making sure they have "ALONE TIME".

Grandma and Grandpa are ALWAYS there!

It takes FRIENDS! Ella, Laura, Grace, Jason, Savannah, Julia, Sheridan, Lexi, Katie

Mommy loves EllaBella

Sisters Laura age 8 Twin Lexi age 6.5 giving the Victory sign!

Laura dances with her Lil Sister

Grandma and Grandpa and Friends
Support United Cerebral Palsy Events!

Ella's Mom and Dad have "Date Night"

Chapter III

Amazing Ryder
Pierre Robin Syndrome/Hypotonia
(Washington)

Hi. My name is Lori, and my amazing son is Ryder. I hope our story can help a family feel better about their diagnosis with their new child. Your life as you know it will change some with any new baby, but with a baby with special needs, it turns you in a whole other direction. I don't mean to scare you. It's still wonderful, but it's just a different kind of wonderful.

When Ryder was born, we had a beautiful eleven-year-old daughter. We tried for years to have a baby, so when I finally got pregnant, we were ecstatic. When we found out it was a boy, we were even happier. My pregnancy was normal. Everything was going to be perfect, or so we thought. The doctor never said one word to make me think things would be otherwise. Later, I found out that cleft palates show up on sonograms. But although I was nearing thirty-five, they never did a late-term sonogram, so they didn't catch it.

I went to my doctor one morning late in my pregnancy, knowing that I still had two more weeks before the due date. But I hoped he would tell me I was ready. He didn't, and I started back to work. On my way back, I was so uncomfortable that I didn't think I could make it home. My lower back was killing me, and the baby was positioned right under my ribs, making it hard to sit and drive. Luckily, my mom was at my house, helping to set up the baby's room. I told her I was in pain but that I'd just seen the doctor, and he said I was still on schedule. In the end, however, we rushed to the hospital, where my water broke within ten minutes of getting in the door.

I lay there for what seemed like forever, waiting for my doctor to arrive. He was definitely taking his sweet time. I had gone natural with my daughter, and when there was no trophy at the end of it all, I told myself that next time I was going for the epidural. So now I asked for one, but I was told there was no anesthesiologist available. It was looking like I wasn't going to get it. I guess I threw a good enough fit that they sent someone in finally to give me some relief. My son was ready to come into the world, but I had to keep holding back. Once he was born, he was blue and was having a lot of trouble breathing. My husband said he looked like a little alien baby.

That's when they noticed the cleft palate, and that his bottom jaw was pushed back, causing a smaller airway than normal. His tongue, which is regular in size, seemed to block it. This, I soon learned, is called Pierre Robin syndrome (PRS), which is when the jaw is pushed back, causing the roof of the mouth not to form properly. They worked on him for a few minutes and then removed him from the room. I have never been so scared, but of course, they played it off like it was nothing. At the elevator, because it was so slow, the nurse took it upon herself to take the baby and run down the stairs to the NICU. Whether or not this was beneficial for Ryder, I still wonder today.

Ryder was in the NICU for weeks. We had to learn how to feed him because having a large hole in the roof of your mouth makes it impossible to suck, and milk would go up through the hole in his mouth and out his nose. Because of this, we were given a bottle with a special nipple, one that we would squeeze into his mouth. Then we'd try to get a rhythm that he could handle. Ryder had to be in an upright position while eating and on his stomach when lying down, so that the tongue stayed down. I used a breast pump for as long as I could—I think for two months—but eventually, I couldn't keep up.

One of my concerns was—what's going to happen when my son starts turning over onto his back? But they reassured me that by then, he would have taught himself how to place his tongue away from the airway. We saw doctor after doctor while we were in the hospital. None of them were very familiar with Pierre Robin syndrome. So we decided that when Ryder did get his surgery, it would be at Seattle Children's Hospital. They had a cleft palate team of doctors as well, who we would see on a regular basis. Even though this was a good two-and-a half-hour drive, we decided it was the best decision we could make for Ryder.

This whole time we were okay, believing that everything was repairable. Ryder would have his palate and jaw surgeries and be a healthy boy, and we were very lucky. A few months later, he did have his cleft palate repaired. I was not prepared for this surgery. I guess because so many are performed, I thought it was a pretty routine surgery. But to this day, Ryder is at high risk when put under anesthesia because of his small airway, so I was more worried about that than the repair of the palate.

Instead of putting him under anesthesia multiple times and putting him at risk each time, we had his palate fixed, tubes put in his ears, and a circumcision all at the same time. Poor thing. I don't think he even noticed the circumcision because of the pain he had from his palate. When I saw him, I just started to cry. He was so swollen, I hardly recognized him. He looked like a chipmunk with a mouth full of nuts. They told us he looked worse than he felt. Even though he was on pain medication, it was still very traumatizing for all of us. He was also given a large, thick tube that went into his nose and down his throat. It would hold his airway open so it wouldn't swell shut.

Ryder only falls asleep on my chest. He slept on a foam pad for a while, but eventually, it was just easier for me to hold him at an angle while he slept. The tube holding his airway open kept rubbing on my chest and shoulder, which was the only place at which he would fall asleep. This would cause the tube to come out. It was horrible to put back in; I was crying with him. My husband had to help hold him down while the nurse placed it. After a few days, when the swelling went down and they felt it was safe to take that tube out, he was given a regular tube for feeding called an NG tube. That tube also went down through his nose and throat into his stomach, but it was much smaller. Before I could even leave the hospital, I had to be able to put that tube in by myself. I'm proud to say I did it on the first try.

It may have seemed bad in the hospital, but once we got him home, he was pulling that tube out every chance got. Usually this was at the worse possible times such as at a restaurant or somewhere in public. That kid wore mitts on his hands all the time.

When we asked about his jaw surgery, the doctors told us that if they didn't have to do his jaw surgery right now, it would be better since they'd only have to turn around when he was fifteen and do it all again. That's when the jaw would be fully grown. Since it was such a painful and complicated surgery, we had his adenoids taken out to open up the airway even more and also to see if he could breathe normally while sleeping. The sleep test—which was quite the experience—turned out fine, so they decided to wait on that surgery. I've always wondered whether, if he did have the surgery, his eating and speech would have come easier to him. They said no, that other kids in his situation were fine with speech and eating.

As he got older, we noticed he wasn't making his milestones. At ten months, we took Ryder to a physical therapist. She said Ryder had a lot of issues that looked like cerebral palsy, but with his clean MRI, we were hopeful she was wrong and Ryder was just *behind*. Then, finally, a doctor noticed that his feet collapsed inward, and he claimed that Ryder definitely had hypotonia or low muscle tone. What they didn't tell us is that this is common with brain damage. However, it did open up a whole new area and helped us understand why he was locking his legs in order to try to stand. Also, instead of crawling on all fours, he was doing this *commando* crawl, a nonreciprocal crawl in which his arms moved in a pattern, but not his legs. Instead, he dragged his left leg behind him.

At five, he now scoots on his bum, but he still has his left leg tucked under him. He will do a 360 in order to keep that left leg beneath him when he turns and scoots. The left side of all of his pants is always worn out, while the other side is good as new.

At about a year old, and just when things couldn't get any worse, Ryder got sick with respiratory syncytial virus (RSV, which is accompanied by high fever). He was put on an IV to give him immediate fluids, and they continued to try and get his temperature down. He was sick and dehydrated, and his temperature would not stay down for very long when he was taken off the medicine. They had to send him by ambulance to Seattle Children's Hospital. We stayed there for a week. They told me that he wasn't getting enough fluids, and with his jaw problems and low body weight, he needed a gastric tube (G-tube) to get food into his stomach, just in case he got sick again. We said, "No way. We'll blend his food to make it easier to handle and thicken his drinks."

They said, "Give him food that he likes, and that will fatten him up." So we did. He ate lots of fruits and pudding, anything to get him eating. We blended it all. We also gave him Pediasure for the calories and the vitamins. Later on, we had to take him to a special therapist just to help him learn to eat other foods such as meats and veggies. The nutritional program was two weeks long, and it took about three days of his refusing to eat and bouts of vomiting, before he finally started trying new foods. What a relief it was to finally have him eating everything the family eats—only blended.

During this time, we found out about Botox injections for drooling. It's popular for stroke victims, and the therapist thought maybe it would work for Ryder. Ryder was going through three shirts a day and had chronic chapped skin. He was a walking, running faucet. We could actually ring out his shirts. We went in to see our ENT, and even though he hadn't done a lot of these procedures, he thought it would be great for Ryder. It worked wonderfully. It lasts about three to five months, and he is so much more comfortable. The medication we tried first, before finding out about the Botox injections, dried his mouth out too much.

The only thing I recommend when doing Botox is that the patient be put under so that the doctor can look at the ultrasound and see exactly where the needle is going into the gland. There are four glands that are injected, and even though the doctor may be able to feel where they are, it doesn't always work. It's best to see, not feel, where the gland actually is. The whole procedure takes about five minutes. The longest part is waiting for him to wake up. Because it's such a fast procedure, it would be easier just do it in the office. But it doesn't always work, and then you just have to make another appointment.

Ryder did get dehydrated again. The doctors believed that he had a seizure in the middle of the night, and that this depleted his fluids. We finally decided to put the gastric (G) feeding tube in for his fluids only. We refused to put his food in the tube and then eventually have to teach him how to eat solids—someday. Even though we have to help him hold his spoon, at least he knows what real food tastes like. I didn't mention that he had acid reflex, so he threw up a lot for the first year and a half. That was a real joy. All I could think was, "There goes three hundred calories."

But the good thing about the G-tube is that it was a wake-up call. It's got me thinking: if they have intense feeding therapies, then what else is out there? I started to research and, wow! Was I overwhelmed! I found out about a therapy called conductive ed—which is a consistent, intense repetitive therapy that concentrates on daily life skills. I researched this for about a year because it's not cheap. Besides, I didn't have anybody telling me, "Yes, this is specifically for your child." This is one of the reasons for this book: to give you some information about programs that actually work and help kids like ours.

I did finally choose a place in Canada, and I saw great improvement in my son. When we came to the center, Ryder was learning to use a walker, but when we left, he was *wall walking* everywhere, supporting himself as he moved by using the nearest wall. How wonderful it was to see him be able to stand and get where he wanted to go instead of being on the floor and having to look up at people all the time. He still scoots on his bum to get places, but for the most part, he wants to be up and moving from one room to the next. I wish I had started him with conductive ed sooner.

The falling issue has been a little scary for us. We definitely have to watch Ryder closely. Because he locks his legs while standing, he cannot get down; and when he falls, he usually goes straight back on his head like deadwood. So no hardwood floors for us! He did try to walk by going from chair to chair, but one fell on top of him and knocked his front tooth out. It loosened the second front tooth too, which also came out within a few days of the fall. Now he looks like Dracula's son!

Ryder and Mom having fun on the quad

Anyway, all I can tell you is *therapy, therapy, therapy!* These children need repetition and even more repetition. The best time for therapy, I feel, is between the ages of zero and seven—the more, the better. I'm not talking about an hour here and there. I'm talking about these intense places that are two to five hours a day, five days a week, for two to five weeks at a time. This isn't something your doctor is going to push you into. This is something you must do on your own.

It would be nice if doctors were better informed about programs like conductive education. When I mentioned it to my pediatrician, he said he'd never heard of it. (More about this in the chapter on pediatricians and their special-needs training).

Here is a program that has changed my son's life, and I feel that the people I rely on to guide me in the right direction are not properly informed. I live on the West Coast, and for some reason, the East Coast is way more advanced. They have tons more therapies for kids with brain injuries. I feel my son has been cheated in many ways because of where we live. You have to push the idea of more therapy and also research what's out there, because no doctor is going to hound you to do it. It's up to you, and you're truly on your own. If you don't have the money, then do your best to find it. This can be done through charity organizations online or in your community. Also, fundraising is great.

Ryder learned a lot of his basics through physical therapy. He has a wonderful therapist that he's been seeing since he was ten months old. However, he was only able to see her once a week, and that's not enough for him. With intense therapy, he was able to learn the same stuff, only much faster.

My sister had a baby five weeks before Ryder was born, and my cousin had her baby one week after. It was fun being pregnant together and talking about everything from food cravings to constipation. We had a lot of laughs. When the babies were born, they were all beautiful, but I couldn't help but feel how unfair it was that Ryder had to struggle with everything he does, while these other babies were thriving. Some of my relatives and friends were afraid to hold Ryder because he had to be held in an upright position, and that made them nervous. Whenever he would make a sound, they would say something like, "Is he okay? Am I holding him right?"

During one family get-together, the kids were playing around Ryder, while he just lay there watching them. It was a break-your-heart moment for me, and I couldn't watch it anymore. I ended up leaving in tears and driving to a park, where I stayed until everyone left. I felt guilty for feeling this way, but I couldn't help it. It was so overwhelming. I later talked to some other moms in a support group I belong to, and they all have had the same experiences. We talked about how simple situations such as a child talking to his/her mom in the store can trigger these emotions. I can honestly say that these feelings get better with time, but they still hit me every now and again. I'm so proud of Ryder and all he has accomplished. He truly is my hero.

Ryder making a funny face while we were taking Madison's senior pictures.

My daughter Madison, who is now seventeen, has had her share of rough moments because she has a handicapped brother. Even though she has done little complaining and we've told her that we love her just as much as her brother, I know there have been moments that she felt less loved. When they are young, it is so hard to convince them that just because their sibling needs more attention, it doesn't mean they are more important to the family. Being older, I think she now understands so much more and is not only a great help but also a loving big sister. We recently took a mother-daughter trip to the city, and I had one of the best times of my life. I so miss spending one-on-one time with my funny, good-hearted daughter. Now that she's a teenager, spending time with Mom isn't quite as much fun; but for me, it's wonderful! When Madison walks into the room and talks to Ryder, he just lights up and gets so excited. I am proud to say she is my daughter. She has something now that I never had as a kid, and that is respect and love for special-needs children.

We still have no conclusive diagnosis. We continue to do genetic testing to see why all this happened. The doctors today have no idea. We have asked for more testing, but it seems we've been put on the back burner. The doctor told us that even if we found a genetic cause, there still would be no cure. To me, that's just a sophisticated brush-off. I now know that with a diagnosis, we might have gone in another direction with therapy. We also might have had more help when it came to insurance.

These days, we're going to a different genetic doctor and continuing to do research. There are amazing procedures out there such as stem cell replacement surgery. We might have looked at them earlier if we would have known more about Ryder's situation.

Our journey will never be over, but I look forward to seeing how this wonderful, special boy will turn out as an adult. So far, he has shown me what love and patience is all about. I am a far better person today because of my extraordinary son.

Ryder at his Nana's Halloween Party

Lori and Ryder visiting NYC for an Intensive Medek Therapy

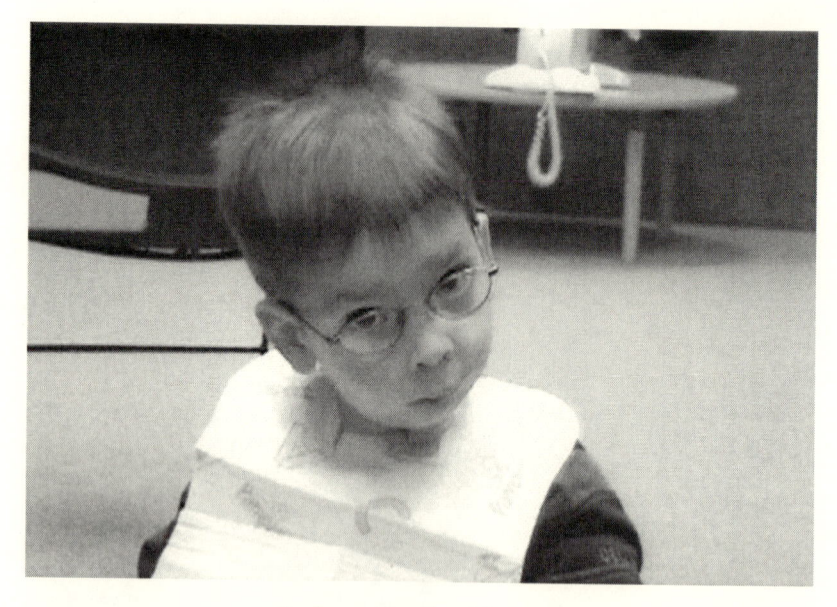

Ryder at Feeding Therapy

Ryder leaving Childrens Village Therapy Center

Ryder and his sister Madison

Ryder hanging with Mom

Ryder with his Nana and cousin Ryan

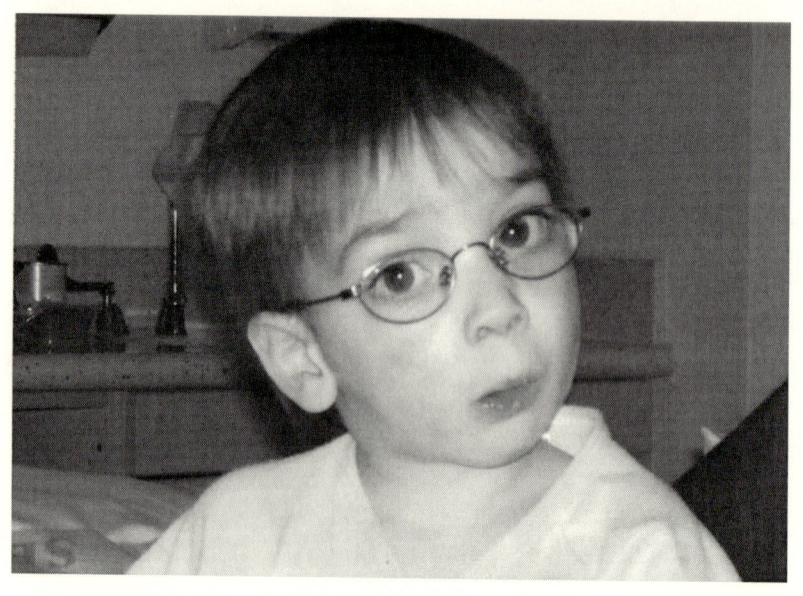

Ryder looking Cute at Children's Hospital just before Botox injections

Chapter IV

Our Precious Fruit
Cerebral Palsy / Hypotonia / Severe Athetoid CP
(Tennessee)

My name is Tina Bonner. I live in a small town in mid-Tennessee, where I have a loving husband named Michael and three children—Ross, nineteen; Seth, twelve; and Rachel, five. We adopted Rachel from South Korea when she was eight months. She has CP, but she's been such a blessing to our lives.

Often, people stop me and are curious. They say, "Did you know she had CP when you adopted her?" I want to answer, "If you only knew..."

I guess you could say adoption is in our family. My sister, Debbie, first adopted two little girls from Russia, and they have been such a joy. I admired Debbie for that and knew she had rescued those girls from an unimaginable life. At the time, my husband Michael and I had been going through a four-year struggle to have a second child. It turns out I had endometriosis. Surgery cleared that up. Shortly after the girls joined our family, I discovered I was finally pregnant. I love children and was so excited. I thought to myself, if we ever want a third child, we'll just adopt. I couldn't take another infertility roller-coaster ride!

As it happened, when my second son was about five and in kindergarten, I began to soul search and tried to decide what I wanted to do with my life. Michael had his own business and was doing well, so I didn't need to work. I had a bachelor's degree in advertising, but I wanted to do something worthwhile, meaningful, and helpful to others.

Michael and I tossed the adoption idea around every few weeks, but we were never serious. At about this time, I was attending a bible study class given by Beth Moore. It was entitled the Fruits of the Spirit. Each week, we studied about the fruit of love, kindness, gentleness, etc. The study lasted several weeks, and the further into it, the more and more I was feeling *led* to adopt. This time, Michael and I discussed the idea more deeply, and we contacted the agency that my sister had used.

We had our first home study, to consider whether or not to adopt, in February of 2005. Everything went smoothly. Money was not a problem. Michael's business, which he'd started in 1988, had been blessed and was quite successful. We decided that a good way to express our gratefulness to the Lord would be to give an orphan a family. Everything seemed *meant to be*. We decided to adopt from South Korea. This was one of the only countries that did not require travel to the site. They deliver the baby to you! Also, South Korea kept accurate medical histories and put the children in foster care rather than in an orphanage.

Before we knew it, we were next on the list. In June of 2005, we were called in to look at pictures and read our new baby girl's story. The whole family went up to the agency together. I told Michael on the way that we should not accept her right away. We should take a few days to decide.

It felt strange to see pictures of the baby. I thought my heart would melt, and I would be instantly in love. But I wasn't. In reading her history, her mother confessed to drinking hard liquor and smoking cigarettes for the duration of the pregnancy. The baby had a difficult birth. She had meconium aspiration syndrome, prenatal asphyxia, and intrauterine growth retardation. She was on ventilator for three days and hospitalized for a month. But the tests they had run since had all turned out normal.

Even so, in some of the photos, the baby had her mouth wide open and her posturing seemed unnatural.

I remember thinking that sometimes, babies do look awkward when they are so young. Then the adoption agent told us that the birth mother had named the baby Bo Ra, which means precious fruit! Awesome! I linked the meaning of her name to the bible study I had been taking when I had felt so led to adopt. What were the odds? We signed the papers to adopt her right there and then.

Adoption takes so long. We had more paperwork, more waiting, and more money to be paid. Each month, our little girl—whom we'd decided to name Rachel—was one month older. Finally, in August, the day after she turned five months old, we got the phone call. At least, I thought it was *the* phone call. Instead, it was a whole other call. I sat in the living room near Michael, while he talked to our adoption agent. It sure didn't sound like he was talking about Rachel's homecoming. The longer I listened, the more I realized something was wrong. Our Rachel was sick or something. When Michael hung up the phone, he said, "It isn't good." He explained that Rachel's foster mother had taken her to the hospital because her arms and legs were stiff. After an exam, an MRI, and a sleep study, the doctors determined that she has CP. She had been started on physical therapy and something called OT.

I couldn't believe it. My body felt numb. I wanted desperately to believe this was not happening. Then Michael said, "The agency needs to know if we still want her, or whether we want to be put back on the list to wait for a healthy child." He said they would put us at the top of the list, and that we shouldn't feel bad because there were lots of people who wanted special-needs children. The agency just needed to know what we wanted to do.

What we wanted to do! What a decision! This would be a true life-altering decision. It would change us, our kids, our family . . . everything. What did we want to do? I could not even talk for a long, long time. I just cried and cried and cried. All my dreams came crashing down. This was not supposed to be part of the plan. Over time, I was gently reminded that maybe it was God's plan! I'd wanted to do something worthy, meaningful, and helpful to others. Adopting a CP child sure would meet those qualities.

Questions came pouring down. Communication back and forth to Korea takes a long time in the adoption world. No e-mails or Internet use. We had to correspond by third-person phone calls and mail! August turned to September, and September to October. During this time, we saw videos of Rachel and had questions answered through mail. We talked to all the doctors and radiologists we knew. Our best source was a friend we had known for over ten years—a physical therapist. She owned a very successful clinic and was personally interested in pediatrics. During this time, God made it quite clear that he wanted us to adopt this exact baby girl. She was so cute in the videos that she was beginning to steal my heart.

Around the end of October, I made the final call to tell the agency that we wanted to get Rachel. Afterward, I curled up in our bathroom floor and wept bitterly. People had told me stories about how other countries said their orphans were disabled, when they really weren't. Maybe this would be the case.

Rachel arrived in Detroit, Michigan, on November 16, 2005. What an emotional day. Finally, I was able to hold her for myself. I was quite surprised because she seemed very normal—not stiff at all—actually almost floppy. The initial meeting went well. Rachel smiled the moment she saw us. There was no sign of the crying the foster mother had commented about so much in our correspondence. The escort who brought Rachel on the plane reported that Rachel had not slept or drank much of her bottle. It had been a twenty-two-hour flight. Maybe I'd misunderstood what she said. On the flight back to Nashville, Tennessee, I tried to give Rachel a bottle from the can of formula that they had sent with her. She wouldn't take the bottle. She fussed and cried on the plane.

Once in Nashville, we needed to drive to our hometown an hour and a half away. When we put Rachel into her car seat, she started screaming. Surely, she would cry herself to sleep. But no! She cried all of the way home. Once we got her out and cuddled her, she was better. She finally took a bottle that night. Her sucking seemed awkward. We laid Rachel in the beautiful baby bed I had created for her. She came alive like we had put her on a bed of coals. Michael worked with her in her room while I lay on our bed, feeling like I was having a panic attack. What have we done? Have we made a serious mistake? I felt our lives were doomed.

The next few days were a blur. We took Rachel to church on Sunday, and our friend Lisa, the physical therapist, examined her. She wanted us to bring her for PT on Monday. During her first PT session in America, Lisa and an OT (occupational therapist) worked with her. They told me they felt that in addition to CP, Rachel had sensory issues and vestibular integration problems. They gave me a brush to use on her hands and feet to help desensitize her so she could tolerate being touched. They recommended that she be swung and tossed around a lot for the vestibular issues.

Thus began the never-ending PT and OT sessions. I usually stayed with Rachel during the sessions so I could learn what to do with her. She could bear her own weight; she just needed help with balance. Lots of help with balance! She hated to put both of her feet on the floor at the same time. They said she did not like that much *input*.

We were introduced to TEIS (Tennessee Early Intervention Services) right away. They help financially and in other ways with disabled children. Rachel was too young to attend preschool system, so someone from the facility came to our house each week to work with Rachel. She had PT twice a week and OT once. At eighteen months, she could attend TEIS's preschool for special-needs children. The classes included some typical children for modeling purposes. I started Rachel there at twenty months. By the third day, I was taking her to school, and she could tell by the route I was traveling that we were headed for school! She was, it seemed, a very bright child! Her whimpering quickly turned to crying. She cried a lot when I took her there, but they said she settled down. She got lots of therapy there, including speech.

At this time I was going to a chiropractor for myself, and when she learned we were adopting a child with CP, she encouraged me to let her work on Rachel. Rachel always screamed while she was there. One day, the chiropractor told me about someone who might be able to help with Rachel. She worked with homeopathic medicine.

I was at the end of my rope with Rachel's crying and inability to sleep well. I decided to give her a try. My sister went with me. She's a nurse. We visited her several times. She used little white balls that dissolved under the tongue. They definitely affected Rachel—sometimes for the better and sometimes for the worse, it seemed. This lady suggested that milk was not settling well with Rachel. We changed her over to Rice Dream. During this time, Rachel did seem to be more accepting of others holding her, and her sleep eventually improved. After a year or so, I started feeling uncomfortable with this lady. She seemed to be using Rachel as a guinea pig, so I quit seeing her.

In PT, the therapists decided to try a Benik Vest on Rachel to help support her trunk. She was also fitted for AFOs—a type of short brace for her ankle and foot. This helped her to not tiptoe as it supported her foot, which she tended to roll out like she was walking on her ankles. Rachel hated the AFOs and went into high tone very badly when she had them on. The therapists kept saying she would get used to them. She was doing well with walking. She was using a Kaye reverse walker. She had trouble keeping her hands on the grips, so they tied them down. Rachel fought that. Shortly before she turned three, her therapist recommended Botox injections. We had mixed feeling about this, but they did keep her from crisscrossing her legs when she walked.

Around this time, our personal life took a turn for the worse. Michael was faced with a horrible situation at work, and he finally had to sell the business that had become such a part of our lives and had supported our family for twenty years. Suddenly, Rachel was only part of our crisis. Financially we plummeted, and life became much more difficult.

The TEIS program lasts until a child turns three. Once Rachel was three, she was put in a new program provided by the city school. They too used normal children in the class to act as physical role models. Rachel seemed to really like school. It provided a very structured routine, which she loves. She received OT, PT, and speech therapy. We ordered her a wheelchair to use during OT, speech, and sometimes in class just to help position her. Generally, Rachel was doing well.

By now, Rachel and I had come to understand each other inside and out, and we adored one another. Still, Rachel could not do anything on her own except roll. I sat on the floor with her to help her sit and play. Hand over hand, I helped her hold toys, move switches, and use a crayon. She loved to try to walk but hated to stand. She often would crisscross her legs while walking. If I held her firmly at her chest for balance, she could bear all of her weight and step with her feet.

We next bought her a Rifton Gait Trainer. This was expensive and not paid for by insurance. Don't even get me started there. She was also fitted for TheraTogs (a newer form of the Benik Vest and a Velcro nightmare).

She never got used to the AFOs. She wore them to school and during PT but not for much else. The wheelchair was not good at keeping her in the proper position. Nothing ever seemed to work perfectly with her. We bought lots of things for her that never seemed to work, while some things that I never expected to work did great for her. I was slowly learning all about love, joy, peace, patience, kindness, goodness, faithfulness, gentleness, and self-control—the fruit of the spirit.

Rachel always had trouble eating. She took her bottle very well and could eat food that was mashed up. She loved mashed sweet potatoes. I would cut up chicken into tiny bits and put them in the potatoes. She also liked tender young sweet peas. At first, I used to hand-pull off the thin shell so she would not choke. Often during a meal, she would choke and occasionally spit up her food. In the winter of 2007, she ended up developing aspiration pneumonia. We treated her at home. During this time, I kept Rachel in bed with me. Michael was away on a trip. It occurred to me that Rachel might sleep better in a big girl bed. I think she felt too isolated down in the baby bed. Sleep suddenly became much better.

My sister recognized that this bout with aspiration pneumonia created a good opportunity to try to get insurance to approve her for speech and swallowing therapy. Until now, they had denied it! Debbie had a friend who was a speech therapist and also a specialist in swallowing. When it was actually approved, she began doing vital stimulation therapy. This helped improve Rachel's swallowing and general oral motor skills. She had always been horrible at letting me brush her teeth, and she has a mouth full of crowns and fillings to prove it. Speaking of this, she had to have a pediatric dentist who put her under to handle this type of procedure. The brushing improved with VitalStim. Rachel's new swallowing/speech therapist diagnosed her with apraxia. She confirmed that Rachel can understand perfectly and knows exactly what she wants to say, but apraxia keeps her from getting the words to come out. She did occasionally spit out a word that was spoken very well. When asked to repeat it, she could not. Frustrating for her and Mom!

By the time Rachel was well over four years old, she was progressing but at a very slow rate. She could not sit alone, stand, walk, crawl, or say any word consistently. Unknown to me, my sister and her husband (the two nurses) started searching the Internet for help. They found a therapy offered in Canada that provided a holistic teaching technique invented in Hungary called conductive ed. This therapy was offered at a place called Ability Camp. They also utilized hyperbaric chamber therapy. The camp was a five-week-long intensive therapy. It was expensive, and it was located in Canada. It seemed an impossibility for us Bonners, given our current financial status. My sister called them to request information. It seemed hopeful. Debbie was not working at the time and offered to attend the camp with me. There was, however, still the money problem.

After lots of brainstorming, a group of family, friends, and church members gathered to form a committee to help raise money for Rachel to attend this camp. Lots of work was involved. We set up a website and a bank account and settled on a fundraiser date, which was just two weeks before Rachel was scheduled to go to Canada. We were people full of faith! The event was called *Be Rachel's Miracle*. Four local artists offered a concert with a variety of music, a silent auction, and a CP adult guest speaker. Hope for lots of donations filled the night. When the event was over, donations totaled $25,000!

Ability Camp was long and exhausting but well worth the money and effort. The moms there opened a whole new world of hope and knowledge for me. I was overwhelmed with information about other therapies available and new ideas. The conductors were very knowledgeable and skillful. Within the first two weeks, they had Rachel walking on a forward-facing walker, with arms extended forward. She needed only minimal help at her hips. She had no AFOs, no TheraTogs, but did use arm splints to keep her arms from collapsing. I learned how to walk her as I sat on a stool behind her. It was work for Rachel and work for me!

The conductors also gave me information on athetosis, which is the type of CP she has. I was able to understand why she moves the way she does and could work with her better than before. The hyperbaric chamber seemed to help significantly. Rachel started babbling more and seemed more alert. Overall, she grew stronger and better in several aspects of her life. She learned to drink from a cup but still used the bottle to get the majority of her liquids.

Once at home, we have seen more improvements with the months that followed. I was most surprised at how impressed her PT was with the results. We have scheduled Rachel to do the TheraSuit therapy soon and want to try Medek also. Intense therapy is definitely a way to see remarkable improvements. Is a return trip to Ability Camp in order? Looks like we need another fundraiser and people who are willing to Be Rachel's Miracle.

Rachel enjoying the summer!

Rachel and Family

Rachel is surrounded by love!

Chapter V

Santosh the Superhero
Autism/Hypotonia
(Ontario, Canada)

It was the summer of 2002, and we were excited as we were expecting one more addition to our family. My older son was five years old then. I had finished school two years earlier and was working in a start-up position. My husband, an accountant, was also comfortably settled. A year earlier, we had bought our first house. It was the perfect time for another child. During my ninth week, we did a CVS blood test, and the results were positive (not good). We spoke to the medical staff, but they weren't very concerned about it.

Our son Santosh (which means "happiness") was born on January 2, 2003, after an eight-hour labor with an epidural. Although I had been admitted at around 11:00 a.m. on January 1, the doctor wasn't available because it was New Year's Day. When she went to lunch, I had only dilated five centimeters, but my water was already leaking. At about 6:30 p.m., they started to induce me, but around midnight, they stopped as another emergency C-section came in. The doc was gone for about two hours. She came back, and they started the procedure. My son Santosh was born at 4:34 a.m. He weighed seven pounds, one ounce, and was twenty-one inches long. He was a full-term baby born at thirty-eight weeks. The first thing I checked on him were his eyes, and there they were—black eyes prying through his long eyelashes—and a head full of dark black hair.

Three weeks before he was born, I had a dream that my baby was visually impaired. I just blamed it on a mother's fear and let it slip by, but it was always there at the back of my mind. After he was cleaned up and brought to me, he had his eyes closed. When I checked with the medical staff, all they remarked was that sometimes the ointment gets into a baby's eyes, and it takes a while for them to open up.

Meanwhile, he also developed jaundice, and they kept him in the incubator under the light. The next day, photographers came in to take a picture, which is common in some hospitals. Even after they tried to get his eyes to open for thirty minutes so they could get a good photo, his eyes remained shut. Again, it was blamed on jaundice and lack of sleep. The hospital pediatrician came in to check on him. No concerns about his eyes, just a routine checkup that indicated everything, including his hearing, was fine. He was not sucking very well, but this was not a concern for them. I was assigned a nurse to follow up with feeding at home, and I was discharged forty-eight hours after delivery.

Once we brought our bundle of joy home, he still was not sucking well, and I started to pump out and give milk to him in a bottle. They called him lazy. Meanwhile, the nurse turned up in our home on the seventh day or so to show me the feeding technique, which I already knew as I had breastfed my older son for eight months. When I casually asked her about checking his vision, she—a mother of three boys—was of the opinion that it might not be possible before a baby is six months old.

We went to our GP (general practitioner) on the sixth day, the second-week, and the third-week checkups, and again, when I broached the subject of his vision, she said small babies always sleep a lot, and she was not much concerned as the hospital hadn't found anything wrong. My *mommy instincts* kept coming back. The third week, which was a cold January evening, when I went in to see our GP, I insisted that she check his eyes.

She was shocked because she wasn't getting any red reflex from either of his eyes. She checked again and again as she had never seen anything like this before. We were literally in tears. My whole world was slipping away beneath me. We can't even recall driving back home. The next morning, our GP's clinic called with an appointment to the town's only pediatric ophthalmic clinic. The eye doctor started his exams, and my poor baby was howling as the doctor tried to pry his eyes open to check them. The doctor confirmed that Santosh had cataracts. It was worse, denser, in the right eye. I was given an appointment to see the surgeon in the evening, and thus began our saga of medical visits, which continues still.

The eye surgeon had a whole team as no one had seen something like this in both eyes, and they termed it as congenital cataracts. Meanwhile, my three-week-old baby was prodded so badly because, as he had such black eyes, it was very hard for them to see. They made sure they had a good look. They'd clip his eyelids, and his cries would tear down the whole hospital hallway.

Surgery was scheduled two weeks later as they had to run some blood work, etc., and also get a *theater of operation*. They would remove his cataracts and fit him with removable contact lenses. Before doing that, however, they had to take a look at the nerves behind his eyes. They'd do this when he was put under for the surgery. They planned to do one eye first and then the other two weeks later. That would give the first eye a chance to heal a bit and to make sure that there was no infection. When we brought him home after the second surgery, he started to throw up. We thought it might be from the anesthesia, but at the post-op the next day, the surgeon informed us that he'd developed nystagmus. This is a condition in which the eyeball keeps moving back and forth. In his case, it was moving horizontally. This, again, was very depressing. What we didn't know was that we were at the bottom of a hill, just waiting to climb up.

Two weeks later, he was sent to the ophthalmologist to get his contact lenses. I would practice putting them in and taking them out. Eventually it became second nature, and I could tell if he had his lenses in or not. In about five weeks, our once-normal life had turned around so much that I was mentally and physically exhausted. The constant in-and-out visits to the hospital stressed out our five-month-old son so much that, one fine day, he woke up with a lemon-sized bald patch on his head. They called it alopecia, which can affect anyone who's stressed out too much.

The routine now was to put his lenses on in the morning when he wakes up, take them off and on for nap time, and then take them off at night. At times, the lenses would fall off, and we would all go on our knees looking for them. I had white sheets over our carpets so we could spot the lenses easily. We lost a few of them as sometimes they would just pop out, and they were pretty pricey.

When Santosh was about six months old, he wasn't gaining weight. They did more blood work and told us everything was normal. Another six months passed by, but he was still not tracking (following activity around him with his eyes). He had very low tone, could not hold his head up, would throw up often, was still on formula, and was only rolling. I just hoped someday it would get better.

We had an MRI booked for Santosh at ten months old. The eye doctor felt that he was actually seeing, but we got it confirmed one day when he gestured toward a toy. When we realized that, we began to stimulate his vision, showing him bright things and wearing bright colors around him. When he was about eleven months, we were approached by Infant Development Services, offering a vision therapist and a physiotherapist. Based on the recommendation of the vision therapist, I started making a lot of black-and-white smiley paper plates, black-and-white checkered boards, etc.

Another thing: from four months on, he started getting ear infections every two months or so. He was treated with antibiotics. He used to gag a lot and had eczema on and off. Shortly after his first birthday, he rolled one step down and he sprained his arm, and again, there was a setback for about a month. Initially, we were seeing the eye doctor every two weeks, then every month, and then every two months. He still had very bad nystagmus and had used and lost more than eighteen contact lenses. I was told they would implant lenses when he turns around four.

We were focusing more on his vision and lying down with him at night. I used to cry for him at night and think, "Why, God, why? What did he do to deserve this? Punish me, but please spare the baby! Please let him be able to see!"

I wondered how I would explain colors, how he would see the sky and grass, and most importantly, how he would see his mom!

By the time he was two, he could sit up for thirty minutes or so with the help of a cushion at the back, but even when he sat, his back was very curved. We went to India for a month, and although it was tedious, I had a good time with my folks. It was very uplifting and really good for our morale! While we were there, the tubes in his ears fell out.

After we came back from India, he was operated in both his eyes for strabismus. He had to wear glasses instead of contacts for four weeks. After this period, he didn't want to switch back to lenses. He'd just pop them out with his fingers, so we just stuck to his glasses. In the fall of 2005, he started preschool at the medical center for medically fragile children. It was thrice a week for two hours, and he got his OT, PT, and speech therapy there. He would sometimes utter a single phrase, and he started to creep now. Still, he was very weak and low toned, and his medications were the same. Now he was under the care of a developmental pediatrician along with a regular pediatrician. He was still below the fifth percentile in height and weight, so he received care from a hospital dietician.

He was shortly going to turn three, and by this time, we had learned about the Institute for Human Potential in Philadelphia, where they run a five-day course for parents of brain-injured children. I attended and discovered that there were some main allergens like soy, wheat, milk, and eggs. I took him off milk and found his ear infections reduced in number. He also tested positive to nuts and was now supplied with EpiPen, which was used in response to severe allergic reactions. On the positive side, we learned the benefits of supplements like probiotics, fish oil, etc.

We started implementing the programs offered by the institute. They were used to stimulate the brain through the various sensory pathways—namely touch, hearing, and smell. We also did cross patterning, which tells the brain how to move, and also did a lot of creeping and crawling. We started a reading program, and after about a month, we could see that he could recognize words.

When Santosh was three and a half years old, we again went to visit the family in India. While there, we tried Ayurveda, an Indian massage. I was still afraid to give him any outside medications, but he was massaged every day. As a result, he transitioned from pureed food to regular food. The massages also helped his problems with constipation and eczema. We stayed in a house full of people, and that helped his social skills. At least, he wasn't crying when someone new came into the house. The trip also helped him get potty trained, which was a big blessing for me. And in India, he started to stand up by supporting himself against the furniture.

After our return from India, we had a dental appointment and discovered that he had an infected tooth. He was put to sleep so that the problem could be corrected and had crowns put on another four teeth. The dentist was of the opinion that he might start to eat better now and maybe put on some weight.

On the physical side, Santosh still was low toned. He now had AFOs, the short shoe braces, and wore them often. We continued with a lot of creeping, and found a program to do with NACD in Utah. We did the program for two years. It followed the IAHP pattern, but it was not as rigid as the institute. Best of all, they could evaluate the child over a video. This program required a lot of effort, so we hired young workers to work with him. With NACD, he started to verbalize a bit, but they discouraged him from standing. Their theory was that he wasn't ready. They were also against the use of any support equipment like AFOs and walkers. Speechwise, he learned to do a lot of signing, some of which were only approximate as his motor skills were delayed.

Now, he started attending a preschool in the community with an aide three times a week for two hours. He was the only special-needs kid there, and it was hard for me to see him go around creeping. He was also the only child there who was not talking or walking.

Around his fifth birthday, he was throwing up. He'd go off to sleep but was easily roused. We took him to the ER. They thought it could be seizures, so he was kept in the hospital for observation for three days and underwent an EEG. Since they didn't actually see a seizure and the EEG showed seizure activities, they decided we could try the seizure medication phenobarbitaol. I got the medication, but we were leaving for Toronto for a week, so I thought we'd give it to him after we came back. We never got to implement it as he was fine from then on.

Around this time, we also saw a naturopath (we had seen several before) who suggested we do parasite, gluten, and casein testing. He came out positive for gluten, and we were asked to refrain from giving him any milk products for a year. That fall, we moved homes. Santosh moved to a new preschool, and I took him off goat milk and oat cereals. He regressed terribly. The once potty-trained kid started to pee everywhere and chew on everything. Suddenly, there was no eye contact and a nonstop stim. I took him to see the developmental pediatrician, and he diagnosed him with autism. I had asked my pediatrician when he was two if he was autistic, and he said he didn't think so, and I'd left it at that.

Just shortly before his sixth birthday, he had a seizure early in the morning that lasted for forty-five seconds. An ambulance rushed him to the ER, where he was checked, and he underwent another EEG. Because it was a one-time seizure, the neurologist did not want to put him on any medication. He was given Diestat, which should be taken should he have another seizure that will last beyond five minutes.

I was literally a nervous wreck by now, perhaps the worst period of my life. I could not sleep at night. I started sitting in front of his preschool after dropping him, not knowing when he was going to get the next seizure. I used to send in chewy tubes and extra frozen cloth in school. They kept giving him these to chew on; otherwise, he'd chew on his hands so badly that he'd make deep cuts on them.

At this time, I was also waiting to see a behavioral therapist from the hospital based on his oral needs. We also saw a homeopath who was quite expensive. I didn't follow up as I wasn't sure about the medication he prescribed. Now along with being developmentally delayed, he was also autistic. I went to some parent workshops to get an understanding of ABA (applied behavior analysis), but our main goal was for him to walk. I was so tired and achy from carrying him around, although he weighed less than thirty pounds.

Around this time, I heard about Ability Camp near Picton, Ontario. It was a five-week camp focusing mainly on physiotherapy, but it also had a hyperbaric oxygen chamber and a conductive-ed approach. This was very effective and a big step for him. After he finished the five weeks of camp, he started to climb up on slides and began to use the walker a bit.

When school started in the fall, he began to walk along the corridors with his walker. He got the *student of the month* for being so competent with his walking. An osteopath recommended that we keep things on his eye level, so we installed lots of shelving throughout the house, with no toys on the floor. We got him to walk as much as possible on the grass and on sand.

Another food allergy test showed that he was reacting negatively to most grains, lentils, beans and soy, wheat and coconut, and a lot of other veggies. We also did a heavy-metal test and found that he was off the chart for minerals.

We implemented a home-based ABA therapy. After initial setbacks, he started to enjoy therapy time and gained a lot of cognitive skills. He was doing well with his walker too, but then, he had a major health setback. He peed blood one day, and there we were again in the ER to check everything out. But again, they could find nothing wrong.

One time, he was playing with his brother and sprained his ankle. When he still could not bear weight on his foot after two weeks, we learned it was fractured, but by then, it was too late to put a cast. So again, he was not able to walk for about six weeks.

After his recovery, we did twenty sessions of HBOT and at the same time implemented the GAPS diet. We also did a listening program, and his speech accelerated. Four months after this, we did twelve sessions of Medek therapy. This GAPS diet, combined with ABA therapy and physical therapy, has been the best so far.

Today, Santosh is a seven-year-old boy. He can walk two blocks without holding hands on the gravel. Although he is still way off the chart for growth, he's talking a lot. He's not fluent, but he is understandable. He is able to differentiate colors and pick up small things out from the carpets. However, his stims are still there. Recently, we did a growth hormone test, and we are still awaiting results.

Over the years, we've done a lot of other therapies too like Reiki, cranial/sacral massage, colonics, etc. The best so far has been the ELISA testing for food allergies and speech therapy combined with music and hippotherapy. For new moms and dads with a special-needs child, I would suggest that you please educate yourself. Join a support group. That helps a lot. In the beginning, it's overwhelming, but as days go by, it gets better and better.

Earlier, I used to concentrate a lot on socializing, waiting for date nights, parties, work, etc. Now, every small milestone Santosh reaches is a big achievement for us. My life has started revolving around him. It's a roller coaster now. First, I used to wait for the moment for him to call me Mom and be able to stand up. Now we want him to talk fluently and be able to ride a bike. The bar is always raised!

Chapter VI

Marykate and Me
Rett Syndrome
(New Jersey)

An Angel among Us

I was sitting in a rocking chair in my family room at three thirty in the morning holding Marykate, one of my fifteen-month-old twin girls. This is how I spent most nights in the winter of 2006. Marykate's sister Kayleigh was usually able to sleep through the night, but Marykate always seemed to be agitated and would wake herself up because of her constant movement.

Marykate and Kayleigh, fraternal twins, were born fifty-six minutes apart on the night of October 20, 2004. They were eleven weeks premature, and each weighed in at just over two and a half pounds. They spent the first forty-nine days of their life in the Neonatal Intensive Care Unit at Lenox Hill Hospital in New York City.

Early on, Kayleigh—who was born second—was the twin who walked the tightrope between life and death on a daily basis. After complete organ failure, extensive fluid retention, and a significant bilateral brain bleed, Kayleigh had emergency surgery at seventeen days old. We were told if she made it, she was at significant risk of having a disability. At that point, I think my husband David and I realized we would have a child with special needs.

Interestingly, during her stay in the NICU, my firstborn, Marykate (who would later be diagnosed with Rett syndrome), had relatively few complications. Marykate's most significant issue was that the oxygen nasal cannula wore away her septum (part of the nasal passage). She would later require plastic surgery.

During their infancy, the girls' growth patterns became erratic. Over the next few months, the developmental abilities of Marykate and Kayleigh grew further apart.

Marykate didn't seem to be progressing at the same pace as her sister. Between fifteen and nineteen months of age, we took Marykate to four neurologists within the tristate area, looking for answers about her lagging development. At the end of every visit, the physicians concluded that she was developmentally delayed due to being a preemie. But as her mom, I knew there was something more going on. Marykate just didn't seem all right to me. After all, Kayleigh, with all of her many complications, was consistently meeting many developmental milestones.

I consulted with my dad, a physician who had completed his residency at Columbia Presbyterian Hospital. He suggested that I make an appointment with one of the neurologists in New York City. My appointment was scheduled for September 13, 2006. The neurologist happened to pass Marykate in the waiting room and saw her hands clasping. He indicated to us at the end of his visit that there was a chance Marykate had Rett syndrome, the most severe form of autism.

First Diagnosed

After we arrived home, my father and I looked up Rett syndrome on the Internet, and Marykate met just about every diagnostic criteria. That was the moment that changed our lives. I didn't need a blood test to confirm the diagnosis, although we later received a positive result. Marykate would probably never walk independently or speak or take care of herself. I went into a depression for two weeks and rarely left my bedroom. When I did venture out, everything around me seemed unfamiliar. My family had hired nurses who took care of the twins during the time that I was unable to function. It was the loss of everything that could be, the dream I'd had of what was to come.

One afternoon while sitting in my kitchen, I got the strength to call the New Jersey Rett Syndrome Association (NJRSA) and speak to someone regarding Marykate's diagnosis. She told me about the traveling clinic and the great strides in research that was being conducted every day for these little angels. I will never forget what else she told me: there are far worse things in this world than Rett syndrome. It was at that moment that I began to heal emotionally . . . and physically. I realized it just didn't matter. Marykate was never going to be on this earth without Rett syndrome. She was either going to be here and have special needs, or not be here at all.

Shortly after this phone call, my state representative got in touch with me. From that moment on I wanted to become involved in IRSE, the organization that gave me the support and strength I needed to continue. When I attended my first IRSE conference last year, I was in absolute awe of the caliber of speakers and the volume of extremely relevant information that was presented.

I also began to look for local resources such as DDD. I found specific recreational programs for special-needs children in Hillsborough, New Jersey. I also found out that in my local school district there was an inclusion-based program for autism and developmentally delayed kids. Our school had great technology and highly advanced science programs. Our local therapists were fantastic and would later all become just like family members.

Starting School and Finding Help

Just transitioning into school was a significant learning experience and, at first, seemed like a foreign language. There are IEPs (individualized education plans), ESYs (extended school year), LREs (least restrictive environment), OTs (occupational therapy), PTs (physical therapy), and related services, inclusion classes, and self-contained classrooms. Where do you turn?

I spent hours investigating the vast number of services on the Internet and quickly learned that no one directory has all the children's disability services listed in one place. As the executive director of EmPower Somerset, a nonprofit company service in Somerset County, I had worked for the Somerset County Department of Human Services on several programs. Now I turned to Somerset County Freeholders and asked for help starting a childhood disability coalition.

They loved the idea, and with the help of parents and professionals, several of them from Hillsborough, we developed the Somerset County Childhood Disability Resource Guide. This simple online directory (*www.childhooddisability.com*) lists all the childhood disability services that serve Somerset County. Education, recreation, camps, transition services, family support, advocacy, and media organizations are now all listed in one place. It is currently being translated into Spanish to reach additional families in our community. Assemblyman Peter Biondi and Hillsborough Committeeman Anthony Ferrera are actively engaged in the ongoing efforts of this coalition, which include events, parent and professional training, and an annual Disability Awareness Day at TD Bank Ballpark, home of the Somerset Patriots.

Organizing a Team

You are the only voice a child has. You need to succeed. You can't give up, you can't fall apart, you can't isolate yourself. You need to do your best, because the future of your child depends on it. The earlier you receive a diagnosis, the greater the chance a child has to have successful interventions. The reality is that at times you will feel discouraged, alone, desperate, and even angry; but your parental instinct will kick in, and your family comes first. The specific challenges of a special-needs child don't just impact the disabled child—they also impact the family, the school, and the community. A child with a disability requires teamwork. Parents can't usually do it alone, and they don't have to.

There are therapists, educators, professionals, and friends on my team. These strong, loving, and intelligent people—who were once strangers to me—became an extension of my family. They have helped us navigate the best course for Marykate, because every child is different, and every child requires his or her own path.

We had to advocate very diligently to get Marykate the services that we have been able to find. We have learned with the help of many others to do things a little differently and be flexible. We have so many therapists and individuals helping us that we soon realized we needed a lost-and-found box in our house.

The Rewards of Your Efforts

Marykate is now in kindergarten at the McAuley School in Watchung. She has her own aide, an incredible teacher, and the perfect school. We are blessed. With a little help, she threw out the first pitch at Disability Awareness Day in June of 2010 at the Somerset Patriots Ball Club.

Marykate is fortunate enough to speak with the help of an amazing eye-gaze computer. The first day she looked at my picture and through the computer said, "Mom, I love you," and she did it again . . . and again . . . and again. I almost cried.

She received a New Jersey Senate proclamation of October 18 in honor of Rett Syndrome Awareness Day, and she was able to thank Senator Bateman through her computer (something I thought was impossible). The computer allows her to share with us what she knows, what hurts, how she feels. It has changed our world.

With my nonprofit experience, I was fortunate enough to work with a group of very dedicated parents and physicians in New Jersey to incorporate the New Jersey Rett Syndrome Association, which opened a Rett syndrome clinic (the eighth one in the country) at Robert Wood Johnson UMDNJ Medical School. Rett syndrome is the only autism diagnosis with a known genetic cause, and therefore, it's thought to offer promise in uncovering the cause of other autism diagnoses.

Last year, DuPont was able to reverse Rett syndrome in mouse research models. My passion is to help families with a special-needs child so their path can be a little easier. I'm especially aware of those who speak a different language or are afraid to ask for help or are without insurance.

I was able to help build the Universal Playground in Hillsborough in October, and I know that thousands of children will now have a place where they truly feel included.

What joy a parent feels when a precious child looks at you and smiles. You know communication is so much more than just spoken words. I look at Marykate's precious eyes and say to her, "You are going to make the world a better place because you are here," and she looks back at me through her eyes and says, "Mom, I wouldn't want it any other way."

What Is Rett Syndrome?

Rett syndrome is a childhood neurodevelopmental disorder characterized by normal early development followed by loss of purposeful use of the hands, distinctive hand movements, slowed brain and head growth, gait abnormalities, seizures, and mental retardation. It affects females almost exclusively.

This disorder was identified by Dr. Andreas Rett, an Austrian physician who first described it in a journal article in 1966. It was not until after a second article about the disorder was published in 1983 that the disorder was generally recognized.

The course of Rett syndrome, including the age of onset and the severity of symptoms, varies from child to child. Before the symptoms begin, however, the child appears to grow and develop normally. Then, gradually, mental and physical symptoms appear. Hypotonia (loss of muscle tone) is usually the first symptom. As the syndrome progresses, the child loses purposeful use of her hands and the ability to speak. Other early symptoms may include problems crawling or walking and diminished eye contact. The loss of functional use of the hands is followed by compulsive hand movements such as wringing and washing. The onset of this period of regression is sometimes sudden.

Another symptom, apraxia—the inability to perform motor functions—is perhaps the most severely disabling feature of Rett syndrome, interfering with every body movement, including eye gaze and speech.

Individuals with Rett syndrome often exhibit autistic-like behaviors in the early stages. Other symptoms may include toe walking, sleep problems, wide-based gait, teeth grinding and difficulty chewing, slowed growth, seizures, cognitive disabilities, and breathing difficulties while awake such as hyperventilation, apnea (breath holding), and air swallowing.

What Are the Stages of the Disorder?

There are four stages of Rett syndrome. Stage 1, called early onset, generally begins between six and eighteen months of age. Quite frequently, this stage is overlooked because symptoms of the disorder may be somewhat vague, and parents and doctors may not notice the subtle slowing of development at first. The infant may begin to show less eye contact and have reduced interest in toys. There may be delays in gross motor skills such as sitting or crawling. Hand-wringing and decreasing head growth may occur, but not enough to draw attention. This stage usually lasts for a few months but can persist for more than a year.

Stage 2, or the rapid destructive stage, usually begins between ages one and four and may last for weeks or months. This stage may have either a rapid or a gradual onset as purposeful hand skills and spoken language are lost. The characteristic hand movements begin to emerge during this stage and often include wringing, washing, clapping, or tapping, as well as repeatedly moving the hands to the mouth. Hands are sometimes clasped behind the back or held at the sides, with random touching, grasping, and releasing. The movements persist while the child is awake but disappear during sleep. Breathing irregularities such as episodes of apnea and hyperventilation may occur, although breathing is usually normal during sleep. Some girls also display autistic-like symptoms such as loss of social interaction and communication. General irritability and sleep irregularities may be seen.

Gait patterns are unsteady, and initiating motor movements can be difficult. Slowing of head growth is usually noticed during this stage.

Stage 3, also called the plateau or pseudostationary stage, usually begins between ages two and ten and can last for years. Apraxia, motor problems, and seizures are prominent during this stage. However, there may be improvement in behavior, with less irritability, crying, and autistic-like features. An individual in stage 3 may show more interest in her surroundings, and her alertness, attention span, and communication skills may improve. Many girls remain in this stage for most of their lives.

The last stage, stage 4—called the late motor deterioration stage—can last for years or decades and is characterized by reduced mobility. Muscle weakness, rigidity (stiffness), spasticity, dystonia (increased muscle tone with abnormal posturing of extremity or trunk), and scoliosis (curvature of the spine) are other prominent features. Girls who were previously able to walk may stop walking. Generally, there is no decline in cognition, communication, or hand skills in stage 4. Repetitive hand movements may decrease, and eye gaze usually improves.

Mom Sharon and Marykate.

Wyatt and Brothers

Chapter VII

Wild-West Wyatt
Spastic Quad Cerebral Palsy/ Hypertonia
(Vermont)

The first time I saw my son Wyatt was through the plexiglass of a transport incubator. I was in a morphine haze, having given birth some hours before. He was bluish from what I could see of him amid all of that medical tape and tubing. He was about the size of my foot if you measured the longest distance from my heel to big toe. I was lying in bed—not in the regular maternity ward, but farther away down the hall from the regular mothers with regular babies. I weakly reached my hand through the hole and barely brushed the wisp of fuzz on his orange-sized head. The transport team doctor was talking and gesturing. Whatever she was saying, she seemed very concerned and earnest about.

For the life of me, though, I really could not keep up with all of the words. It was dark outside, and I was trying very hard to figure out exactly where I was. I knew for sure that I had made an emergency trip to the hospital that morning, and the last thing I remembered seeing was two doctors on either side dressed in official doctor clothes with those little hats and even those face masks on. One had a scalpel in her hand. Another doctor was sitting next to my head about to put a mask on me. My arms were at either side—IVs, tubes, lights, and sheets. Come to think of it, the doctor with the knife, my doctor, was talking just like the hazy one standing before me now. She too seemed very concerned.

Well, not too long after that, the fog cleared—at least for a while. The situation was more than a little concerning. Wyatt had been transported to another hospital. I had this visual image of his little incubated body going into the Star Trek transporter that vaporizes all of the molecules of your body, propels them through space, and by some phenomenon of science, reconfigures them all in another more desirable location. In actuality, the transporter was a far more mundane device, an ambulance traveling at a mere 55 mph max over a really big mountain with a really windy road and at least two deadman curves. The more desirable location was an NICU in a bigger hospital a few hours away, probably with a whole staff of concerned and earnest doctors.

Wyatt had a traumatic birth that morning. He was born at twenty-eight weeks of gestation at a birth weight of just under two pounds. His delivery was by emergency caesarean section—a big, long incision from my navel to my pubic line. That morning, Wyatt's placenta had abruptly separated from me, causing me to lose a good portion of his blood supply, and mine. I had seen it—the blood—that morning, a scary volume of it. I had gotten myself to the local hospital, confident that the miracle of hospitals and doctors would—in a rational and professional set of practiced procedures—stop this terrific bloodletting, give me a set of instructions which I would follow to the T, and tell me to go home and get some rest. All of that sort of happened, but the bloodletting needed to stop. My blood pressure was dangerously low, and Wyatt was in severe distress. There was no time.

The practiced procedures of a hospital emergency were implemented. Quick questions, short answers, concise conversations, efficient nurses, and directions . . . everyone was following directions. While I was lying on the table in the OR, just twenty-five minutes after having arrived in the hospital, I rolled my head to the right and saw through the glass of the OR door that my husband had made it. I rolled my head back to center to see the earnest and concerned doctors, and I felt myself fade from consciousness, all squishy and floaty, as a mask was placed carefully over my nose and mouth. The doctor on my right talked to the doctor on my left and then started to count back from ten.

Within minutes, Wyatt was lifted from my abdomen and whisked out of the OR to the waiting pediatrician. I know this only because my husband told me. He watched them through the glass window of the door as Wyatt was lifted and stood aside from the swinging doors as he was whisked through. Wyatt breathed on his own for a minute or so, I guess before the little alveoli at the bottom of his lungs got all stuck together and could not expand. The sticky spongelike masses that capture the air's oxygen and direct it to the bloodstream did not have the surfactant needed to stop them from sticking together. Wyatt could not breathe on his own.

The first attempts by the local medical team to intubate him were unsuccessful. He was too little, they did not have enough experience . . . it's hard to say really what happened. They couldn't get the tube down his tiny throat to his lungs. He was sucking wind. He was "air bagged" for a long period as they waited for the arrival of the transport team from the closest hospital with a NICU. The transport team had been called shortly after I arrived at the hospital—one of those concise phone calls in the practiced emergency procedure.

When the transport team arrived, Wyatt was intubated. He had already suffered severe respiratory distress. The transport team could not stabilize Wyatt, and it was several hours before he was able to be transported. Hence the darkness when they arrived in the morphine haze of my hospital room on their way to the ambulance. The two-hour trip to the NICU was extremely difficult for him.

Late that night, I received a phone call in my hospital room. Wyatt's NICU doctor had a foreign accent. It was a very professional, calm, and warm voice that delivered the devastating news. It did not look good. Although Wyatt had survived his trip across the mountain, he was suffering severe respiratory distress and still was experiencing incredible difficulties; he was not breathing on his own. His little heart was wildly unstable; his brain had suffered oxygen loss; his kidneys, liver, and all the other essential organs were traumatized. The doctor said he would call back tomorrow.

I am not sure how I found the phone cradle after that. I fell back onto my bed feeling the nausea of medication and sadness wash over me. The nurse came in after a bit, stroked my arm, and placed a dry cloth under the side of my face to absorb the tears that were pooling between my cheek and the pillowcase. She added the next dose of morphine to the IV, and I felt the stinging warmth as it flowed up the vein in my arm and slowly brought an addictive numbing release to all that hurt.

The next several days for Wyatt were all about survival. I was unable to travel to the NICU as I recovered in the hospital from this horrific slit through all the layers of my abdomen. My family and friends vaulted into help mode. My husband made daily trips to the NICU, my two older sons were collected by my sisters and mother and brought to Boston, my church congregation started cooking and delivering meals, and I started to pump breast milk. Tiny Wyatt struggled on, each day cycling between settling a little teeny-tiny bit into his new incubated surroundings only to crash again. He remained intubated for the first several weeks. I remember praying one night while still in the hospital for God to send his angels down to the NICU. I imagined all these sweeping robust angels with powerful wings perched around Wyatt's incubator, gently and firmly blowing air in and out of his lungs. Deep breath in, and now a deep breath out. I thought that I could will his lungs to maturity.

Well, it was me, the angels, and the earnest staff of doctors who—thank goodness, by the modern miracle of science and hard work—were saving premature babies and sending them off to a full, productive, and healthy life. I often chide myself for not remembering to tell those angels while they were doing all of that good breathing to grow new brain cells into Wyatt's head, the ones that stopped firing when he wasn't breathing. I wish I hadn't had so much morphine when the doctor called me that night. I might have remembered to give those angels the correct request.

The first few days turned into a few weeks, and the few weeks into a few months. In addition to being premature, Wyatt was extremely physically immature for his gestational age. They took the tube out his lungs at three weeks of life as his lungs started to function. He graduated to a nasal CPAP—forced oxygen through his nose and then to his nasal cannula, breathing oxygen on his own.

Wyatt remained in the hospital for a little over three months, struggling. His weight gain was slow. He had extreme difficulty digesting anything, including the gallons of breast milk that were now stored in my freezer and in those of my friends' and neighbors' as well. He was on a nasal feeding tube for the entire period. His development was very slow, and he suffered low heart rates and blood oxygen desaturations throughout the period. He really never became alert during that period.

I spent as much time as I reasonably could at the hospital, traveling back and forth daily or staying overnight in the hospital. It was extremely stressful on my family. My husband returned to work and took care of the home front. My two young sons, Wyatt's brothers, missed our normal family life, and while we had explained things to them as simply and straightforward as possible, they watched me carefully. They queried often, as children are wont to do when they sense that something is gravely wrong and the adults are trying to protect them.

When he reached five pounds, the doctors said we could take Wyatt home. It was a celebration of sorts. We had hit the magic number. Wyatt was sent home on oxygen and with a nasal feeding tube, an oxygen monitor, prescriptions for medications, a referral to the VNA, and a list of phone numbers. His five head ultrasounds showed no significant brain damage, which gave the doctors and me such hope that—while Wyatt had had a rocky start—things were going to be okay. The doctor with the foreign accent and calm, warm voice hugged us and said, "You are one of the lucky ones! Take him home and take care."

So we did, back over the mountain in the dark of a winter evening in the middle of an icy snowstorm. My husband and I nervously traveled, negotiating both "deadman" curves and letting months of air expel from our lungs as we figuratively wiped our brows and said, "Whew! That was a close one." We believed then that we had narrowly saved Wyatt and could go forward with our lives, grateful that we were not one of the unlucky ones.

Wyatt had a very hard time at home. He cried and slept and barely ate. I nursed him or fed him small amounts of breast milk through his NG tube. I fed him 5-10 ml (1-12 tsp) fifteen to eighteen times a day. He slept most of the time, and when he was awake, he was often irritable and very stiff. I slept with Wyatt for most of this time. He settled into my elbow, and I kept myself awake trying not to move a muscle so as not to wake him. I kept thinking that he needed to sleep to grow and get on with the wonderful life he had ahead of him. I loved him and held him and sang to him and walked him.

Within a few weeks, it was apparent to me that he was not progressing well, and he was also very uncomfortable. My pediatrician, the good man who had tried to intubate Wyatt in the hospital, really was out of his realm. He gratefully referred us to specialists. Over the course of the next several months, Wyatt was diagnosed with gastroesophageal reflux, bronchopulmonary dysplasia, retinopathy of prematurity, and cortical vision impairment.

An MRI at five to seven months showed significant brain damage. It turned out all those head ultrasounds were wrong, and no one had been motivated to do a CAT scan while he was at the NICU. Now he was diagnosed with severe periventricular leukomalacia (PVL) with a resultant diparesis (gigantic holes in the white matter of his head). One sympathetic neurologist dumbed it down for me—a lot of traffic going on in his head but no highways for it all to travel on. Genetic testing also showed that Wyatt had Williams syndrome, a chromosomal disorder that—along with characteristic low IQ, heart issues, and joint problems—exhibits with a bonus cocktail party personality. I had not yet actually observed any of this partylike personality, but I clearly remember rebuffing the sympathetic pity from one tangential and overly concerned caseworker who indicated that she knew how devastated I must be with yet another diagnosis on top of everything else. I laughed, clearly advising her that she knew nothing about how I was feeling and that, obviously, she wasn't Irish—because if she had been, she would know that anything that involves cocktails has to be a good thing. She later apologized to me for making assumptions, and I to her for my inherited biting wit.

We tried various medications for reflux and BPD. Ultimately, I weaned him from all of these because they either did not work or had very bad side effects. Based on the results of an EEG, Wyatt's first neurologist—a man who was an expert on brains but not conversation—advised me that at eight months, I should put Wyatt on a strong anticonvulsant medication. I sought a second, third, and fourth opinion and opted not to use the antiseizure medication. At twelve months, Wyatt experienced the onset of a serious disorder called infantile spasms, a devastating global electrical malfunction in the brain. Our pictorial neurologist described this as akin to an old television whose antennas do not work—they just receive shades of gray screen static and a lot of buzzing.

It took several weeks to get the spasms under control, and we treated them aggressively by ultimately using the drug Vigabatrin, which was not available in the United States. I had to drug run, with the aid of friends and a well-known commercial carrier from a pharmacy in Canada. The doctors had provided me three drug options: one that had an extremely low efficacy (translation: will not work), one that would likely cause permanent liver damage and would work only slightly better, and one that had about a 70 percent chance of working but would likely cause blindness while he was on it. All three of the drugs suppress the brain activity, so Wyatt's already global development delays would be even more globally developmentally delayed. Without any drug, his brain would be an electrical mess—likely forever. We chose blindness and the best chances.

I hit the lowest of lows emotionally at this time. We had gone from being "one of the lucky ones" to something very different. We were able to stop the spasms after four weeks. Wyatt remained on the drug for one year, and then we gradually weaned him. During that year, he was also shown to have cerebral visual impairments, and he was diagnosed with cerebral palsy. I remember that New Year's Eve as we welcomed the new millennium. I was so flipping happy to say good-bye to the stress of the previous months. I was so prepared and willing to work hard to do whatever I could for my little boy, so hopeful for science.

Wyatt has made slow but steady developmental progress. He is a very happy boy who loves people and loves to communicate with people. He has been working on the Medek PT program for seven years and is able to hold his own weight. He can sit on a chair and, for a short period, on the floor unassisted. He does not crawl. He can walk somewhat with assistance but generally has limited ambulation. Still, he is progressing. I work with him and play with him daily to help him progress physically.

Wyatt has had a *big* growing year. It seems he somehow went from being a little boy to a big boy while I was not looking. Wyatt turned ten years old at the end of 2008. It's so hard to believe; he's come such a long way.

Wyatt keeps doing things that I do not expect. Having had no experience with children with his particular disability and personality, I can only gauge by what I know from typically developing children. And like so many topics, I learned enough to know that I have so much more to learn.

In walking, Wyatt is progressing all the time. He's still not walking on his own, but he's oh so close. We hit a serious plateau last fall and could not seem to move him to the next step. Then over the winter, with some great help from his personal aide Catherine, and his physical therapist Kate (and I think some maturity in his brain), he learned to hold up his own weight. He *wants* to do it now. We do the same exercises over and over and over, and it seems that finally his brain gets it and says something like "Oh, I'm supposed to stand!"

I can only compare it to my mother when she was older and became sick. She needed someone to lean on when she walked, to give her balance. At some point she could not hold herself up anymore, and that was the point where we could no longer help her walk. She needed to hold her own weight. It was just not possible for us to walk with her if she did not. Well, Wyatt's ever-maturing brain finally got that. He is readily holding his own weight, and we are more and more giving him balance. But he is up! He tires easily, but he keeps trying. Now all the time he is telling us, "I want to do standing!" in restaurants, in church, in the house with visiting friends, etc. It is a ridiculous amount of work for us because he is so big and heavy, but so far, we have enough brute strength around here to work with him.

Wyatt's hearing is amazing. He can distinguish all types of sounds and words. He can hear airplanes and motorcycles long before we know they are even close. It is almost like having radar. Unfortunately, that also makes him hypersensitive to sound. Noises from mixmasters, hairdryers, blenders, vacuum cleaners, and the like really bother him. Noises from barbershops, dentists, and clapping and cheering pretty much send him over the edge. He does love music and singing and listening to books.

Wyatt's language has exploded. He loves to listen to books and repeats the phrases from them all the time. The fun part is that he uses language appropriately! He still loves *The Cat in the Hat* and *Green Eggs and Ham*, but we are trying to expand his horizons. He also picks up phrases from listening to people and is repeating things all the time. This is good and bad. He was in church during the summer when he commented quite loudly, "Oh my god!" It sent a few ripples of giggles through the pews. With his improved language development, he has gotten quite clear about telling us all what to do and what he wants. So now we are learning patience and manners. His vocabulary is huge, but sometimes his diction is hard to understand—it usually takes a while to get used to it.

Wyatt continues to be a very happy boy. He loves people and all his friends, young and old. Communicating with people is his greatest pleasure. He gets so excited when anyone comes to visit or we go visiting!

Wyatt Sitting

Happy Wyatt

Happy, hardworking mother of three special boys.

Wyatt loves his brothers!

Part II

EDUCATIONAL PHOTO GALLERY

Aunt Lois Sings with Ella "Take me out to the Ball Game"

"Ella in a Wind Tunnel" live life have fun

Ella and Lexi and Big Sister Laura Celebrating their Summer Birthdays

Ella wears the DMO suit for sensory intergration and Ataxic Movements everyday to decrease movement and tone

Tamara (Ella's mom) talking to Fox News about the importance of "Disability Rights"

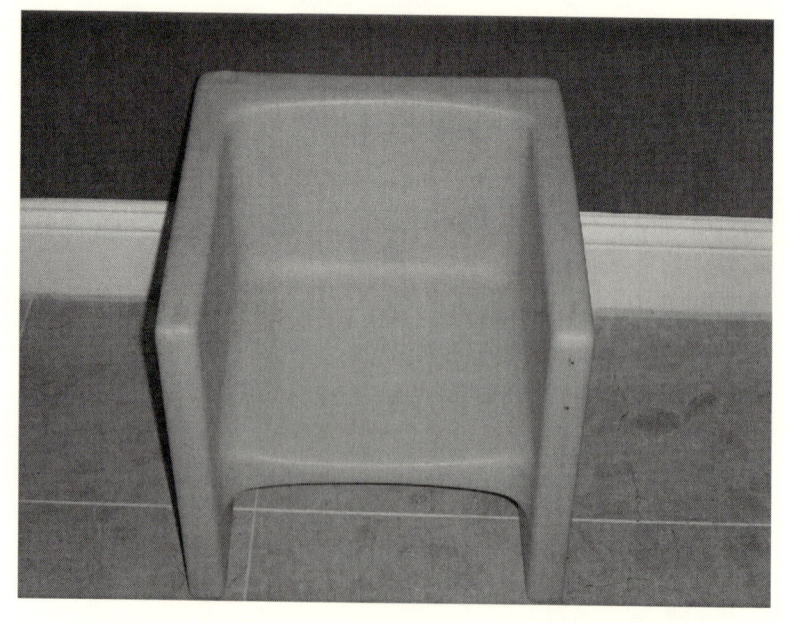

"The Cube Chair" Great when learning balance and stability!

You could apply for "Make A Wish"
to have a Disney dream come true!

Ryder with his NG tube

Ella wearing special prism glasses, Benik Suit, and Benik hand supports.

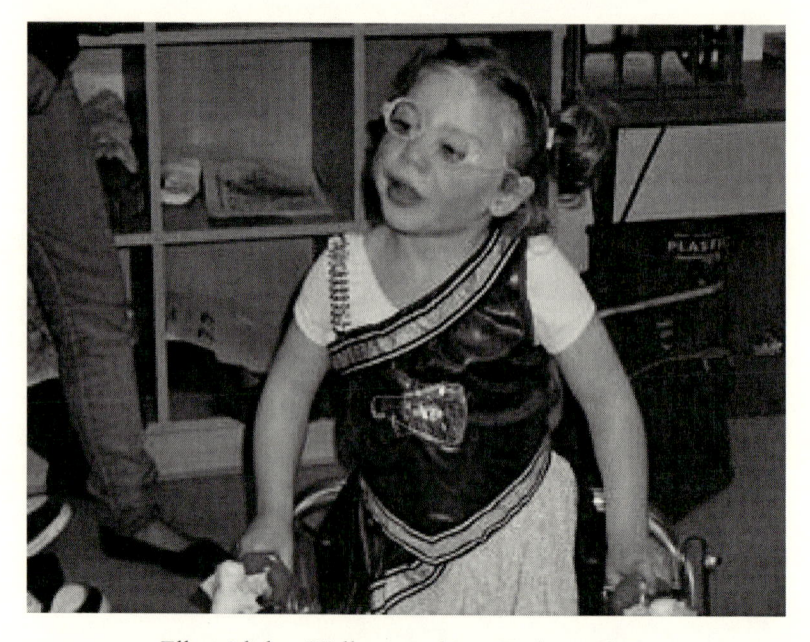

Ella with her Walker age 4 in a Fashion Show

Ell'a Sleep-Safe Bed

Ella loves "Disney" for Special Needs kids

Nanny Sonia communicates with Ella with Sign Language!

Sister Lexi understands Differences!

Ella's Friends Nina and Jake from PG Chambers School.

Rachel on Horse for Hippotherapy

Rett Syndrome fighting for a cure, but living with hope!

Conductive Education materials

More Conductive Education materials

Work hard, play hard!

Adaptive gymnastics, soccer, ballet classes are available!

Ella's with her dad, Alan, and Governor Chris Christy

Donations and fundraising by local and city organizations are so helpful for sponsorship of kids and therapies

It takes a Village! Jordan, Laura, Rebecca, Lexi, Ella, Emily

Ryder on adaptive bike

Ryder with The Kids on The Block Special Needs Puppet

Ryder Loves Camping

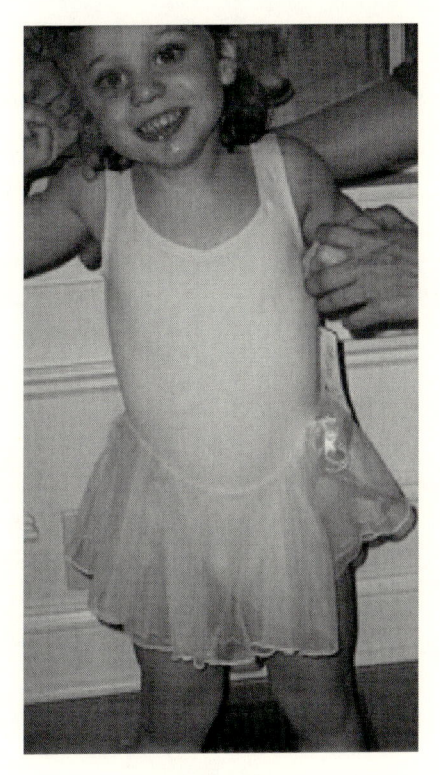

Adaptive Ballet

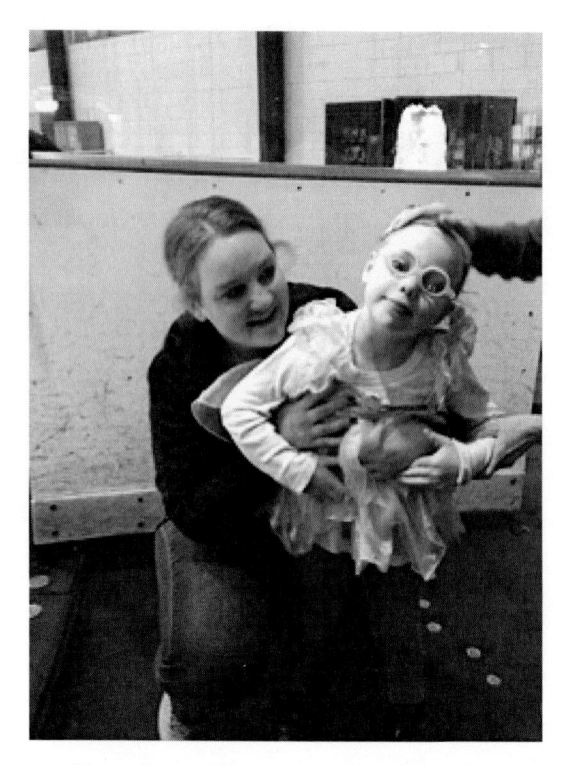

Ella with Ice Skating Coach Andrea from BSA just learning to stay up on Skates. Go Ella!

Example of a "Sensory Room" in a house

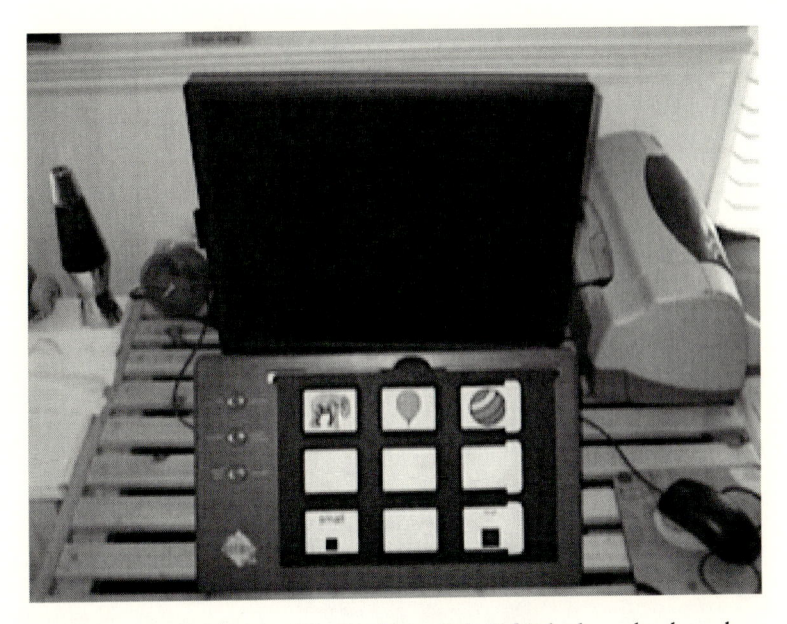

Intelli-Keys bought by the Warren Twp. Bd. Of Ed. they also bought our Dynovox! They really do care.

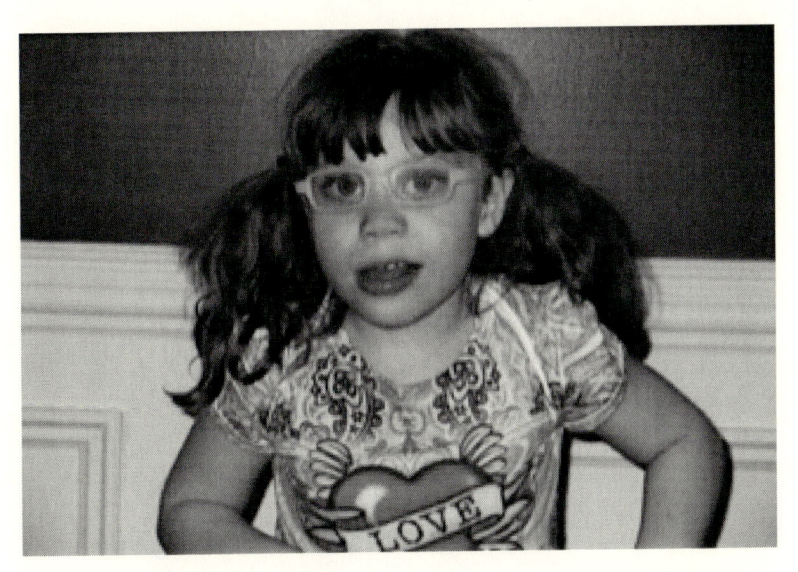

Ella in her "Flexi-Glasses" they are created for Soccer and other Sports. They are so flexible and Ella keeps them on her face.

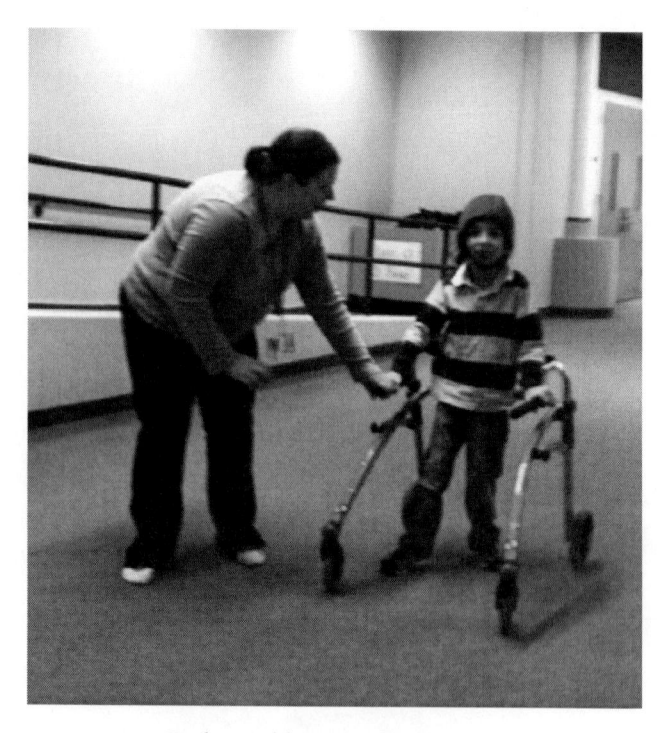

Ryder and his Amazing Speech
Therapist Amanda Having some Fun

Here's to Ella and Mom for completing the
2nd round of Auto-Genius Stem Cell Therapies!

The good old "Trip Trap Chair". The Warren Bd. Of Education also got Ella one so she could be "included" at school for lunch with her Aid miss Mary Russo

Take all your kids on field as much as possible!

Ella's Mom finds joy with Friends and Girls Night Out!

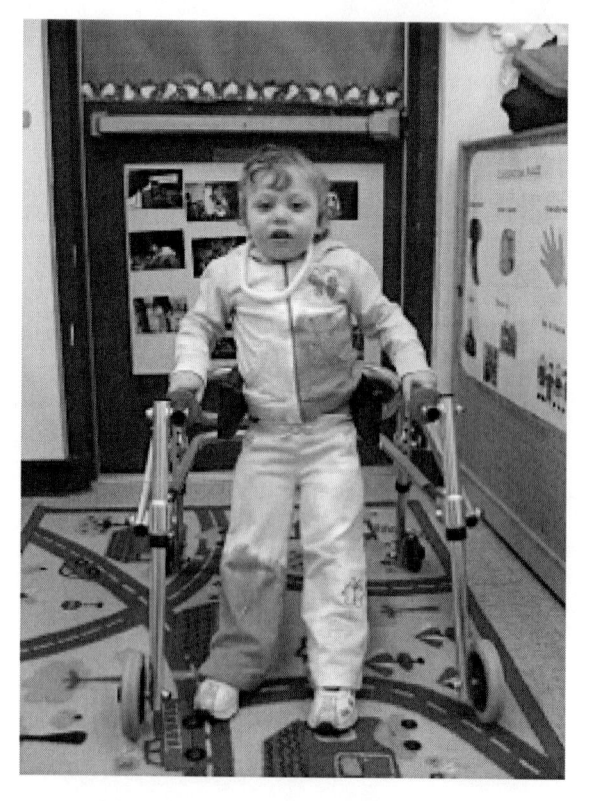

Chewy Necklace and Kay Walker/She has come a long way

Ella in Hippo Therapy

Ryder using a Felt Board at School

Ryder during Hippo Therapy with PT Karla

Ryder at a Special Needs Skating Party

117

Part III

A Cocktail for Success

Okay, everyone, here's what you need to know about therapies:

Basic OT (occupational therapy), PT (physical therapy), and speech therapy are just the beginning. You must look into so much more. There are special category names under the general titles of OT, PT, and speech for severely impaired kids. For example, there's Medek PT, TheraSuit PT, and treadmill PT, to name a few. Under the broad title of OT, there's conductive education for fine motor and daily living, sensory therapy like brushing, swing and vision therapy, feeding therapy and oral motor clinics, and prompt therapy for speech. These regular protocol therapies are okay for learning disabilities and some low-hypotonic children. However, a severely injured brain needs a different treatment plan altogether.

Yes, occupational therapy is very important. Yes, speech therapy is very important. Yes, physical therapy will be your life for many years. But what specific kind of therapy? Where? How frequent? How much money will this cost? And what do I do now?

These questions and answers can't be laid out in any one book. As two moms, we just want to document the journey. We share with you what we feel is absolutely a cocktail for success for a child growing up with severe cerebral palsy as well as many other traumatic brain disorders. We don't claim to be doctors, lawyers, or neurologists.

If the state provides you with one hour of therapy a week in each area (speech, physical, and occupational therapy), those three hours are not enough. You need to kick it up many, many notches. Don't let any doctor or school board or case manager of any kind tell you what your child's limitations are. Your child has already been cheated. Now you need to give your child as much therapy as he/she can handle. The more you demand, the more you'll get. The community, the local school system, the state, and insurance companies all want to save money and provide you with as little as possible. They're not interested in what is best for your child but rather in spending as little as possible to keep you off their backs. They're not mean-spirited; they're just strapped for funds. Always! What your child actually needs cost a lot. So you need to insist! And just because your doctor isn't pushing more therapy, that doesn't mean your child doesn't need it!

You only have a limited window of opportunity to make a significant improvement in building connections within the brain. According to Piaget and Dr. Erik Erikson's stages of development, your best opportunity for learning is between the ages of zero to three. It's still effective for ages three to five. You can even make some significant progress between ages five to eleven. We don't mean that children don't continue to develop; it's just that the growth will be at a slower rate. That's why you need to be a warrior. Very young children are like sponges for soaking up new information. Also, in those early ages, one area of the brain seems to take over the function of the one that is damaged. And isn't that exactly what you want to happen?

Chapter VIII

The Neo Intensive Care Unit (NICU)

The NICU may be necessary, but it is one scary place! Having a baby in the NICU for any length of time means long days and nights of fear and hope, and lots of praying. No one understands the bond that parents of long-term NICU babies feel toward that baby. It is one of the following, "Oh god, why me?" "Help me!" "How can I go home when things are this bad?" "What aren't they telling me?"

But no matter how much time you commit to this child, you feel absolutely powerless, and that feeling is universal. Perhaps the child cannot latch on and be breastfed. Perhaps the child is seriously premature. Perhaps something is wrong with an organ. Maybe the baby is struggling to breathe. Whatever it is, you have such a strange feeling knowing that your child would die without this advanced technology and dedicated nurses and doctors. Thank God we live in the twenty-first century, right?

The NICU has very tiny babies. The smallest we saw was ten ounces. We tried not to stare or listen to his cries. These babies are on tubes and monitors and have staff constantly monitoring machines. You learn that the word *apnea*—sleep apnea—means sleep deprivation. If your baby has cerebral palsy or other forms of brain impairment, you also learn about dysphasia, cleft palate, jaundice, gastric reflux, de-sating, caffeine, and PVL. You learn all these medical definitions because you're going to be dealing with them for a long time.

"Failure to thrive" babies are babies who are not growing at the appropriate rate due to many different conditions. Most of the time, they need NG or G-tubes to give them formula and other nutrients. There are cases where a baby's head has stopped growing. An inappropriately small head is called microcephaly. An enlarged head is called hydrocephaly. In the NICU, they measure the child's head and weight daily. Many babies require an NG tube because they aren't able to suck or are unable to hold down formulas. This condition is called reflux. Getting nutrients through tubes is something nursing staffs work on daily at the NICU. Eventually, the NG may prove to be ineffective. Therefore, a G-tube is placed directly into the stomach.

Muscle Tone

It's very overwhelming and scary when you're hearing words such as hypotonia, hypertonia, dysphasia, or apraxia, and you don't even know what these words mean. The first thing you need to do is familiarize yourself with the words that describe your child's shortcoming. I strongly suggest that you spend time on the computer—perhaps Google the words. When you understand a word, it becomes less mysterious or frightening. You'll have an understanding about what help your child will need in the areas of speech, gross motor skills, fine motor skills, and cognition, or thought.

Okay, now you've learned the words. You know approximately what you'll have to deal with, and it's kind of like being at war on five fronts. You have to think about where to best send your resources. If this was a military action, and you found yourself surrounded, where would you send your men? You would deploy tanks to one front and maybe send boots to another. You'd have people striking from the air on the third front. Well, think of the *cocktail for success* as a military action for a moment. When you're in the NICU and start hearing those trigger words, it's like a military action. You need to tool up, man up. Get to the Web and gather ammunition. To study your enemy is to learn how to beat your enemy. So toughen up and think like a soldier! Remember, you're fighting for the most important thing in your life: your child!

Advice for parents with regard to the NICU

If your baby is placed in the NICU, try to get to know as many of the nurses as possible. They are really the first line of defense. Nurses aren't really supposed to tell you anything, but you can ask them direct questions or read the concern on their faces. And anyway, you see the nurses a lot more than you see the doctors. When they let you know something is really wrong, that means you need to go to or call in a developmental pediatrician or a pediatric neurologist, etc. There is always a reason when your baby has to stay in the NICU, because hospitals like as quick a turn over as possible. If you have to keep the baby in the NICU longer than you expected, you can be sure that the problem is serious. It's a real signal that something is out of whack. Doctors and nurses don't take or say these words lightly.

Many hospitals offer parent support groups. These may be "just what the doctor ordered" to help you get through such a trying period. Take advantage of the opportunity to learn from others who are further along in the process.

The NICU is really a waiting game. It's emotionally exhausting. I hated that the nurses were feeding my baby, and not me, and I felt guilty whenever I wasn't there. But I also forgot to take care of myself. Don't let physical distress follow emotional distress. You need to be strong and healthy for your baby.

I wish I'd have known that, so I could mentally have prepared myself for what my journey would be like.

Every big hospital has OTs, PTs, and speech therapists on staff. They work with babies to try to get them to take a bottle, to help manipulate their swallow, move their tongues, etc. Also, they identify problems with hand grasps, with body tone, with reflux, and a myriad of other problems.

Hospital Social Workers

Although my daughter was in the hospital for more than three months, I did not know she might be entitled to Social Security and Medicaid. It just didn't occur to me. Then someone said to me, "Isn't there some rule that if your baby is in the hospital for more than thirty days, you're automatically entitled to Medicaid?" I later found out this was true. However, I was just learning the ropes. And as it turned out, we didn't qualify for Social Security or Medicaid.

Every NICU has a social worker willing to talk to you. That person is there for you! This social worker, who is usually on staff, has one primary focus: to make sure you're aware of what's available to you and what your rights are, fiscally and otherwise. A major advantage of making an appointment to see the social worker is that he/she has been through whatever you can imagine, and then some. But no one can tell you *specifically* what it's going to be like. Now, of course, there are many hundreds of thousands of children who spend time in the NICU. Most do not end up with cerebral palsy or other traumatic brain injuries. However, there are many children who do suffer PVL brain bleeds in the category of one, two, three, and four. Category one is often mild, but by category four, you're up to a collapsed lung or cardiology problems.

When my NICU experience was over, I thought, "I'm bringing my daughter home. We're going to be okay. We'll learn how to use the suction machine." The wires didn't scare me anymore. I'd learned to change her diapers despite her feeding tube, and I knew how to feed her through her G-tube—which at this point was inserted above the belly button—in a simple procedure. We could handle this, right? But it didn't take much more time to realize we'd oversimplified. What we soon realized was that our journey was going to be pretty darn complicated.

Our speech teacher in the NICU!

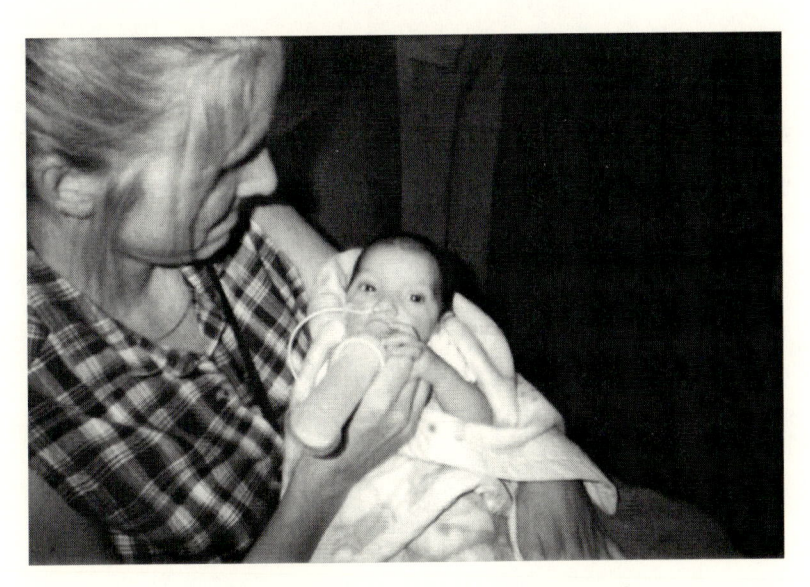

Lori feeding Ryder at Childrens Hospital

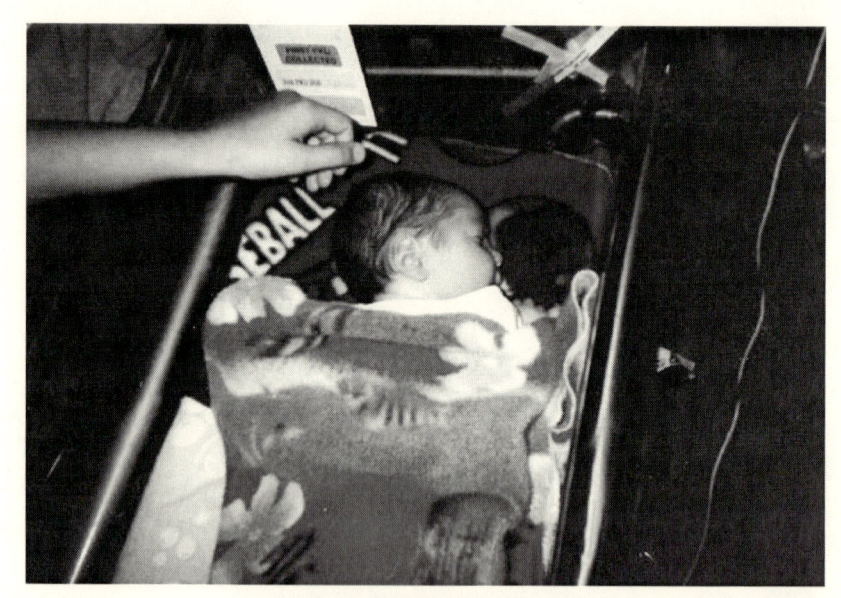

Ryder 2nd Day in NICU

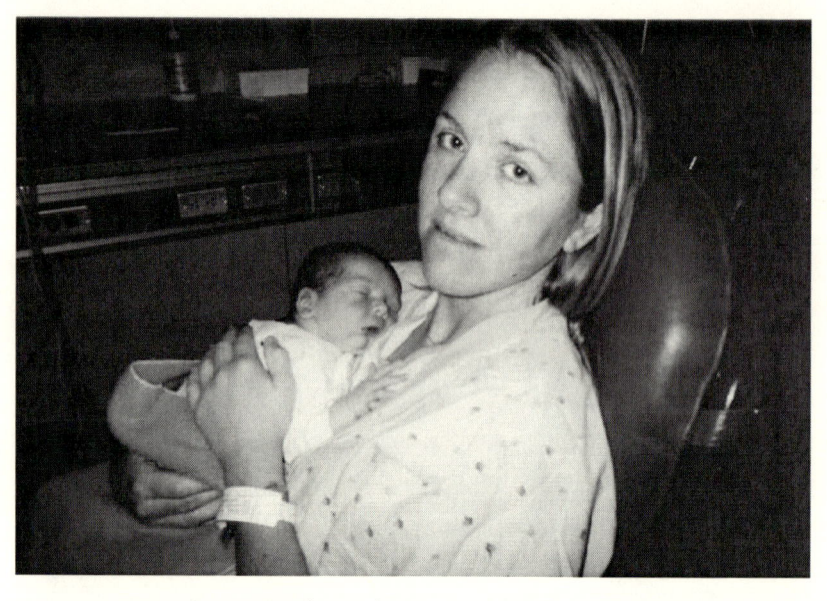

Ryder and mom in NICU

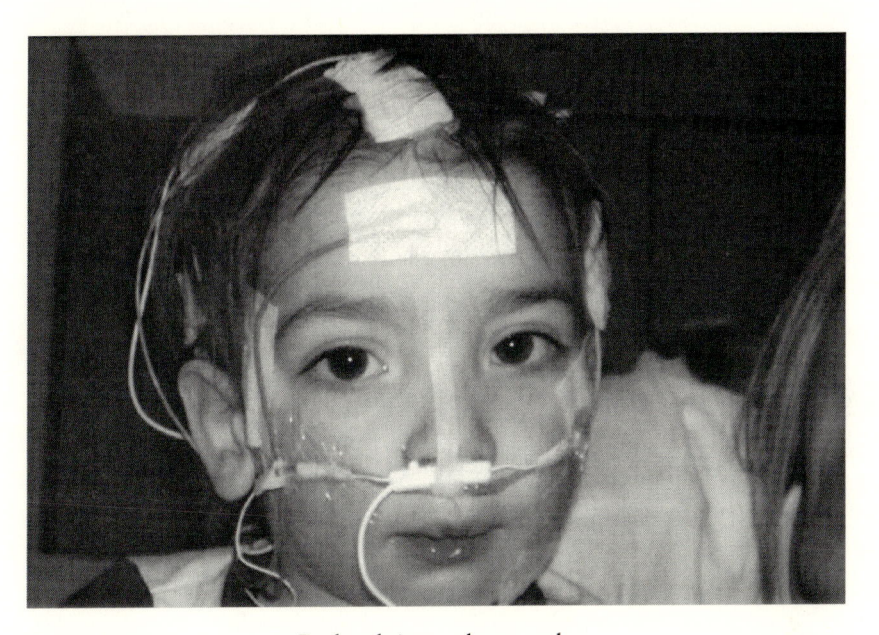

Ryder doing a sleep study

Rachel and Cole at Ability Camp

Chapter IX

Conductive Education (CE)

We want to share a little history of conductive education—what it is and how it was brought to the United States.

In 1968, a professor named James Hari from the University of Wisconsin went to study conductive ed at the Peto Institute in Hungary. He brought back his knowledge to the States. A year later, in 1969, another professor in the same university, Dr. House, heard of the Peto Institute. He signed a contract to develop and work with what was to be called the IMC project, which involved twenty children disabled with cerebral palsy or CP in the state of Wisconsin. Soon after, three American women decided to devote ten months to the Peto Institute in Budapest to observe, learn, and bring back information to the States.

The University of Wisconsin was supportive of this research. It paid the expenses that enabled Dr. House to evaluate the Hungarian approach, which had as its goal the integration of life skills into the training of special-needs children, especially those with CP. By 1971, Dr. House had reached conclusions and published studies regarding the Hungarian method. Then he left the IMC project, turning it over to Dr. Laird Heal.

Early in the 1980s, Dr. Alexander Russell, a pediatrician who worked in London and Jerusalem, brought *Spastic Society* publications by Ester Cotton with him to a meeting of the International College of Pediatrics in the USA. This was the first time that most of the other scientists had heard of the programs in Hungary and Wisconsin.

In 1985, the International College of Pediatrics held its forum in Budapest. They decided to visit the Peto Institute for themselves. Dr. Frida Spivack, director of the Kingsbrook Jewish Medical Center in Brooklyn, was impressed enough by what she saw to invite Peto Institute's director, Dr. Maria Hari, to New York City. By then, the institute was famous, and it sent one of its *conductors* to the United States to live in Brooklyn while developing and working with the first true conductive education (CE) program in the USA.

In 1987, the New York City Board of Education introduced the concept of conductive education to its special education classes. By that time, New York City had many years of experience with special ed classes for a variety of physically handicapped and mentally and emotionally challenged students.

Slowly, conductive education began to make its way across the Western world.

In 1988, two workers for United Cerebral Palsy of New York received a grant from the World Rehabilitation Fund (did you know such an organization existed?) to observe conductive education in both Australia and Hong Kong.

A year later, United Cerebral Palsy introduced a modified CE program in a preschool class in the Bronx. A team approach was used, and it was staffed by a school psychologist, a physical therapist, a classroom teacher, a special ed teacher, and several assistants.

In 1990, the First World Congress on Conductive Education held its meeting at the Peto Institute. Jerry Lucas (director of program development for the Ontario March of Dimes) attended, and CE has flourished in Canada ever since.

In 1991, the Brooklyn Chapter of UCP hosted four Hungarian conductors who helped train and develop leaders for the CE program. Ester Cotton, the psychotherapist and recipient of the Honorary CE Award, gave a big workshop at the Matheny School in Peapack-Gladstone, New Jersey (just a few miles from Ella's house).

In 1992, the Inter-American Conductive Education Association (IACEA), which was formed by Dr. Spivack, began to disseminate information and training around the country. In 1993, a group of parents of special-needs children organized a CE summer program. Meanwhile, in Trenton, Ontario, an experienced OT named Vicky Tsang started a CE preschool program. (Other programs have been developed and begun all around Canada and the USA. Find information about them on the Internet).

It was 1995 when a year-round program called Ability Camp began in northern Ontario, Canada. It was founded and directed by Kevin Hickling, who himself was the parent of a handicapped child who was enrolled as a patient at the Peto Institute. Hickling Sr. was so impressed that he was determined to bring conductors of CE full time to Picton, Ontario. This school/camp continues to exist today. It was at this camp that the authors met one another as well as many other parents who brought their special-needs children to Picton from around the US and Canada. Can you believe that between the authors' children, Ella and Ryder, they have attended the camp a total of seven times and, each time, were amazed by the improvements the kids made, thanks to the dedicated instructors: Ms. Tunda, Ms. Kristina, and Ms. Brenda.

Living in an all inclusive environment, we feel, also educates the parents on what's expected to help these kids in their learning. With no outside interferences, parents are able to concentrate on their child's therapy and needs with plenty of time for play as well.

As parents, we feel that conductive education takes negative behavior and converts it into something positive. In addition to the underlying brain damage, children can develop laziness, such as refusal to self-feed or walk, because it's so hard, and because it's become accepted by the family. If these bad habits and behaviors are tolerated, the child will never develop to the extent that conductive education (CE) deems possible. CE addresses these issues with children ages zero to three, three to five, etc. The child's program is tailored to the child's individual ability and age (seven to nine, ten to fourteen, fifteen to adulthood). CE pushes *each child* to accomplish as much as possible in the way of everyday life activities, such as potty training, walking, dressing, and eating.

Begin this form of daily living with your child, and you can improve the child's ability to function, develop, and learn in the real world. The name of the game is survival. Here we will share some important concepts about CE with you:

Kids do better with things in their hands. There are thousands of sensory receptors in your fingers alone. Try to have your child keep something in his/her hands as much as possible. This might include objects such as rings, baskets, balls, sticks, and jingle bells.

Grasping bars are used to assist in self-feeding. You can purchase these at IKEA, Kmart, etc. Most are attached to suction cups and can be used when traveling with your child. This real-wood grasping bar is screwed onto a plinth.

Chairs are used for balancing and gripping. A special table called the plyth is used to help a child to pull and push his whole body. Brain-injured children were not given the opportunity for proper development in utero, or suffered oxygen depletion during or after birth. We need to do more for them than for other children to make up for that deprivation. And we need to place them into as normal a learning environment as possible.

Time is a definite need in conductive education. You need time for therapy that focuses on each specific daily life skill. For example, how a child gets out of bed should be consistent and repetitive at all times. Stretches are a good idea each morning. The belief is that with the same exercises each day, the kids will improve with their body tone, which will help develop independent physical life skills.

Both of our children attended Ability Camp in Ontario. During this time, over the course of two years, we have come across extremely experienced conductors. Here's what our children accomplished: holding their heads up, pulling and pushing, development of wall walking (walking along holding onto a wall is preferable to not walking at all or being in a wheelchair). Some self-feeding, semi-potty training, climbing (especially in the playground), independent and speed of walking, and the motivation to become more independent. Once these kids were up on their feet, there was no going backward. While attending Ability Camp, not only did our kids receive top-notch therapy, but also they, and we, have made lifelong friends.

We may be from around the world, but we all share the same goals, dreams, and experiences. For example, if you were at a Wal-Mart or at Micky D's, and your child projectile vomits, your CE friends would not even think twice as you help clean up their clothes, shoes, and the floor. Or if you're at a restaurant and your child pulls things down from the walls or off the table, or randomly walks up to other people and pulls their hair when your back is turned, even though you'll get an evil look from the waitress, your CE friends will just help you retrieve the guilty child, smile, and apologize to victimized restaurant diners.

When parents of special-needs children who attended Ability Camp would be asked about what would bring the fastest change among all brain-injured children, this would be their response: "Conductive education is a godsend." Another way to receive CE, that may be an extra cost would be to have a graduated Peto Institute instructors come into your home, or you stay at a hotel while attending an institute, or stay with friends or willing residents near the camp. We recommend that you google CE where many websites will appear, and you will find a list of available conductors hosting their available dates. In Israel, England, Hungary, Russia, and China (to name a few)—find the center that is suitable in terms of cost and location, and let it work for you!"

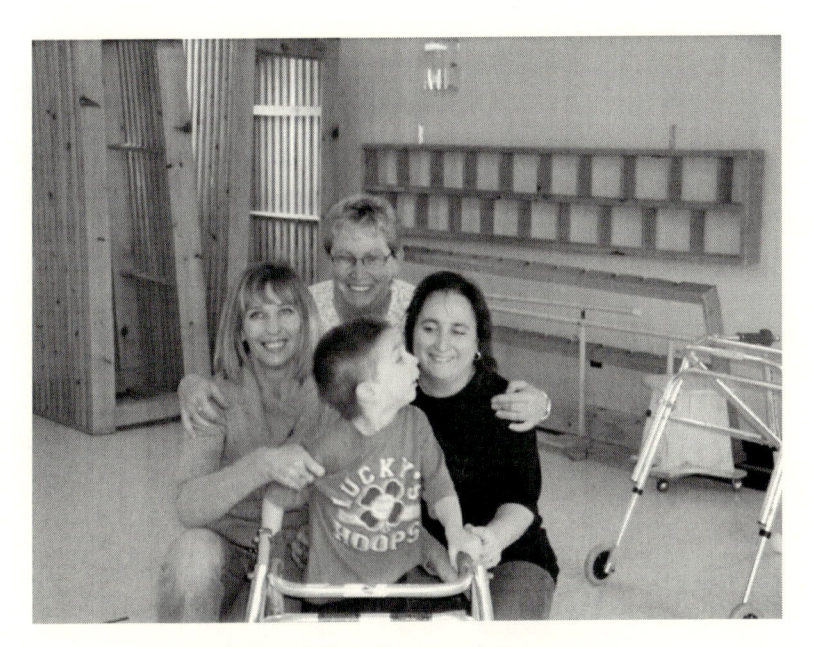

Ryder at Ability Camp with Instructors:
Ms. Tunda, Ms. Brenda., and Ms. Kristina

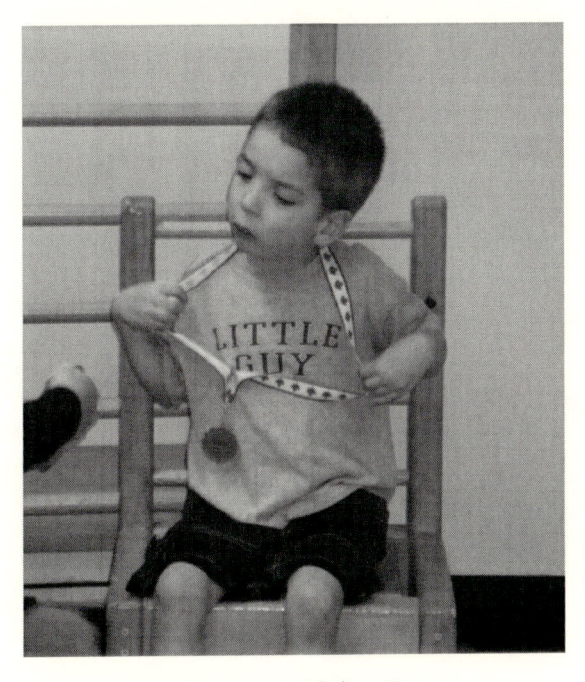

Graduation at Ability Camp

Ella during a Conductive Education session

Conductive Ed Classroom

Chapter X

Physical Therapies: NDT, MEDEK, and SUIT THERAPY

We strongly acknowledge that NDT (neurodevelopmental treatment) which is basically traditional American physical therapy, is wonderful. However, you get the greatest impact if the child participates in several forms of physical therapy rather than just one. A multifaceted approach is the way to go.

Of the several different types of physical therapy available, one of the least familiar is Medek, and yet it is one of the most powerful for long-term improvement. How do we describe Medek to a parent? Medek is a pediatric rehabilitation therapy. The approach is based on dynamic, challenging exercises applied manually to a child affected by developmental motor functions. This approach provides concrete guidelines to stimulate the child in a totally safe way, starting at two months of age and continuing for many years after birth.

The CME therapy concept was created and developed by the Chilean physical therapist Ramon Cuevas. CME is an acronym composed of Spanish words. In English, it translates to something like *The Dynamic Method of Kinesthetic Stimulation*. We simplify and just call it Medek, or its newer name, CME. Santosh in Toronto, and Wyatt in Chile, worked with Medek practitioners, while Marykate, Ella, Ryder and Cole have all worked with the New Jersey practitioner Azriel Novogroder, who is very highly ranked and respected. In Medek, the therapist keeps pushing the child's limitations, using distal manipulation and/or wooden boxes, beams, and wave boards to stretch a child's abilities. Once the child can achieve success at a therapy session, with continued repetition, he/she will eventually be able to replicate the success at home and in public.

In our conversation with Azriel, we learned a lot. He explained that CME aims to provoke children's brains to have automatic responses, which will allow for greater functional motor control. It exposes various body segments to deal with a gravity system that fights against the child's brain and skeleton. It challenges the child's neuromuscular system in order to force the appearance of (non obvious) motor functions. It integrates *range of motion exercises into global function activities.*

Azriel and his beautiful family.

Neither hypertonic (high tone) or hypotonic (low tone) conditions are a limitation for the use of CME therapy. During a CME session, a child's emotional irritability such as crying is a totally acceptable reaction. It's not an impediment to treatment unless the child completely shuts down.

However, says Azriel, there are times that one can deal with the brain and body but neglect the child. His job is to be *ahead of the child but not leave him too far behind*. It's as though you were on a motorcycle. You've got to move the gears ahead, but then you've got to know when to pull back.

For this therapy, the child's intellectual disabilities are not necessarily a limitation. The child can use the exercise program only. Cognition, however, can only enhance the rapidity of the learning. Speech isn't a limit to this therapy either. Kids with any degree of developmental motor delay caused by cerebral palsy, any hypertonic condition, or a motor-delayed condition caused by any nondegenerative disease are great candidates for CME. Azriel thinks each day about ways to make his children do most of the work and not rely on him to do it for them. A favorite quote is, "How can I let go today?" He uses a tap or a touch to guide.

We asked Azriel, "How would a new client know whether his/her child is a candidate for Medek?"

Answer: You do a four-week trial, or at most, under certain circumstances, an eight-week trial. At the end of that period, you ask whether the child shows improvement in that area."

He continues: "Physical therapists aren't meant to fix kids. We are meant to help bring them to a maximum level of their function. I keep my feet on the ground, but I'm reaching for the stars."

When he deals with older children who spend all or most of their time in a wheelchair, he tries to encourage them to use all of their body when doing exercises. "Don't forget your legs," he'll say. "Don't leave them behind." He laughs and tells us, "I use all the tools in my tool belt."

If you can find a Medek practitioner, try for one who is level 3 or above. If this means traveling globally, so be it. We recommend Azriel Novogroder if you're in the Teaneck, New Jersey, area. He's a level 4 therapist who knows how to build up the core and the trunk. The bodies of impaired children are weak in general and have major signal problems (apraxia). Through repetition, these signals can be forged and repaired. We are talking about years of repetition, not months or days. Sorry!

TheraSuit Therapy

We've already stated that you get the greatest impact if the child participates in several forms of physical therapy rather than just one. TheraSuit PT, also known as the Adeli suit, is another successful therapy.

In 2002 a device called a TheraSuit was created by Richard and Isabella Koscielny, who are physical therapists and parents of a disabled child. It's meant for children with CP and traumatic brain injuries.

Suit therapy is now used for the experimental treatment of children who have cerebral palsy and other traumatic brain injuries. However, the families in this book who've participated in suit therapy don't think it's experimental. They all had great benefits from this therapy. Suit therapy is a modification of a space suit called the Penguin Suit, which was used by Russian cosmonauts to counter the effects of long-term weightlessness on the body while in space. The inner workings of the suit have elastic bands and pulleys that create artificial force against which the body must work to help prevent muscle atrophy. Just think, parents. You can pretend with your child that they are real astronauts. The suit is used for positioning and stretching the muscles during physical therapy. Suit therapy for CP is currently available in Eastern and Western Europe and is very popular in many states all over the US.

The suit consists of a vest, shorts, kneepads, specifically adapted shoes with hooks and elastic cords that help tell the body how it's supposed to move in space. Therapists use the suit for the proper physical alignment of the body. During specific exercises, therapists take the elastic bands and tightly connect them to the mirror flexors, extensor muscles, trunk rotators, and the lower limbs. So if someone asks you where the kids are, you can say, "They're all tied up in therapy."

Additional attachments correcting the position of the feet, head, and other areas have also been designed. Suit therapy consists of various exercises that demonstrates to the child how walking and balancing are supposed to feel, establishing patterns. Also, suit therapy can help a child "learn to fall," so that instruction takes the place of missing reflexes. A treadmill can be included in this type of therapy. United Cerebral Palsy funded two studies using anecdotal and verbal reports, both of which found suit therapy to be beneficial to children with brain injuries and CP.

Ella sees a fabulous physical therapist named Jennifer Inglit in Morristown, New Jersey. Jennifer is a trained doctor in NDT and PT and chooses to study and implement PT for severely impaired children with traumatic brain injuries while they are wearing the *suit*. She feels this increases the amount of speed with which a child can develop a new skill. Ella has completed four three-and-a-half-hour, five-day-a-week sessions and three-week intensive suit sessions. She carries this over one day a week for two hours throughout the year. She has worn the suit for one and a half hours each in the three-hour sessions.

Ella performs treadmill therapy and other challenging PT exercises like climbing ramps, walking on mattresses, and going through obstacle courses. TheraSuit has increased Ella's rate of speed in walking, given her great protective reflexes, built up her muscles, and given her core strength. It has helped straighten her gait as well. She also wears bungee cords, which allow for the child to have dynamic movement while practicing backstepping, sidestepping, and Yoga-like positions, in total safety. For part of the time she might glide head up, and forward and back in the *spider cage* with cords holding her up. The spider cage gives her the ability to jump up and down and swing side to side and back and forth, which would otherwise be impossible for a child with CP.

Typical TheraSuit exercise goals consist of counteracting muscle atrophies, improving strength and development of highly functional movement patterns, and preventing joint contractures. The definite benefits of suit therapy are as follows: it provides proximal stabilization of the trunk, provides deep pressure proprioception, provides tactile and vestibular stimulation, retrains the central nervous system, restores ontogenetic development, normalizes muscle tone, gives dynamic correction, provides development of fine and gross motor skills, and improves speech production.

The typical cost of a three-week session could range anywhere between $2,000-$5000. There are many trained PTs in the country who now implement suit therapy within their practice.

Other forms of physical therapy include hippotherapy, which is horseback riding geared to strengthening the trunk of the body, increases balance. Most of the time, hippo is taught by an occupational or physical therapist. The therapist uses visual cues, such as flags, to indicate to the rider to do such things as stop/go, speed up/slow down, move side to side, or forward and back. In some cases, insurance will cover the costs.

Then there's aqua therapy, which is taught by a physical therapist. It is perfect for stretching and exercising without putting too much stress on underdeveloped musculature. This is because the child is buoyed up by the water. Anything from a hot tub to an Olympic-sized pool can be used. It may also be covered by the family's insurance policy.

With these therapies, your child will come a long way. You will be amazed at what they can accomplish. With CME, suit therapy, NDT, aqua therapy, and hippotherapy, a child who was told would never walk, has hope. Miracles can and *do happen*. Do the time, and reward is on the way.

Balance Ella, you can do it!

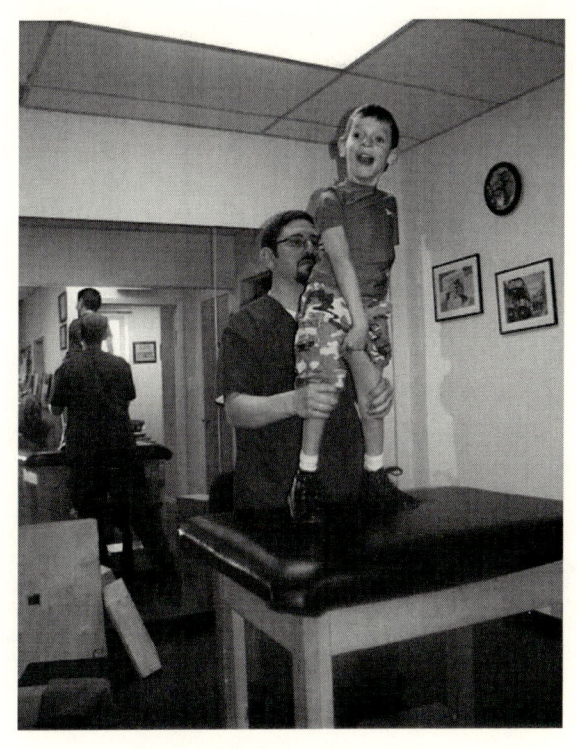

Cole in Medek, Jan 9, 2012.

Ella finishing Aqua-Therapy. Teaching,
keeping your mouth closed and blowing bubbles!

Ella in Medek, Jan 9, 2012

Ella, age 6.5 during Hippo Therapy

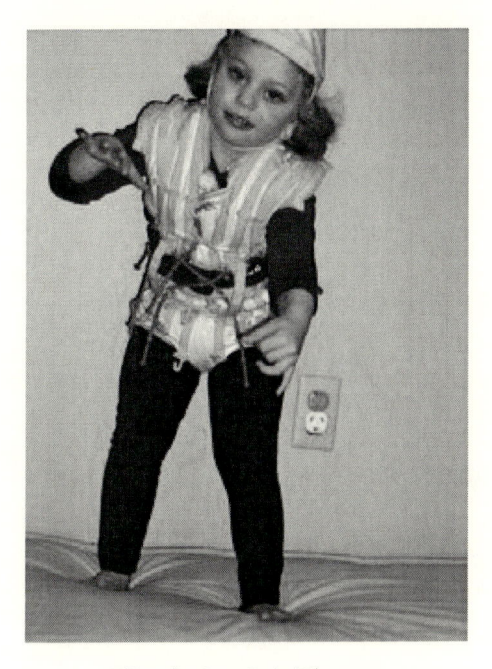

Ella, during Suit Therapy

Ella, with teacher Jen during Physical Therapy

Ella . . . Walk!

Ellaat Suit Therapy

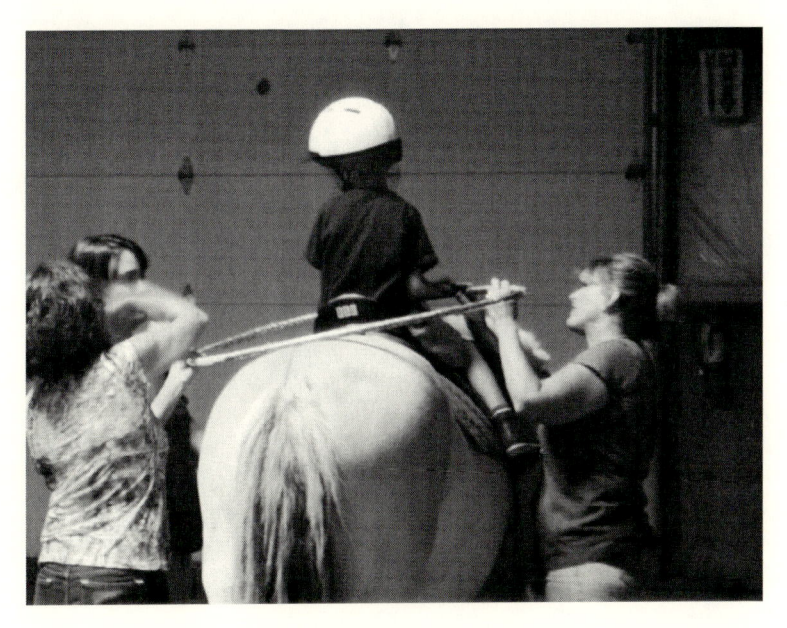

Ryder at Hippo Therapy

Ryder, during Hippo Therapy

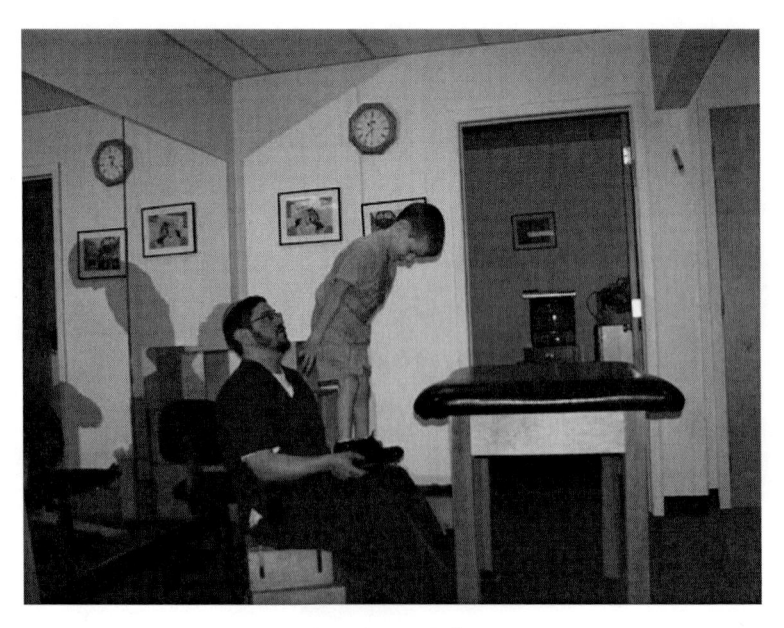

Stand Up Cole!

147

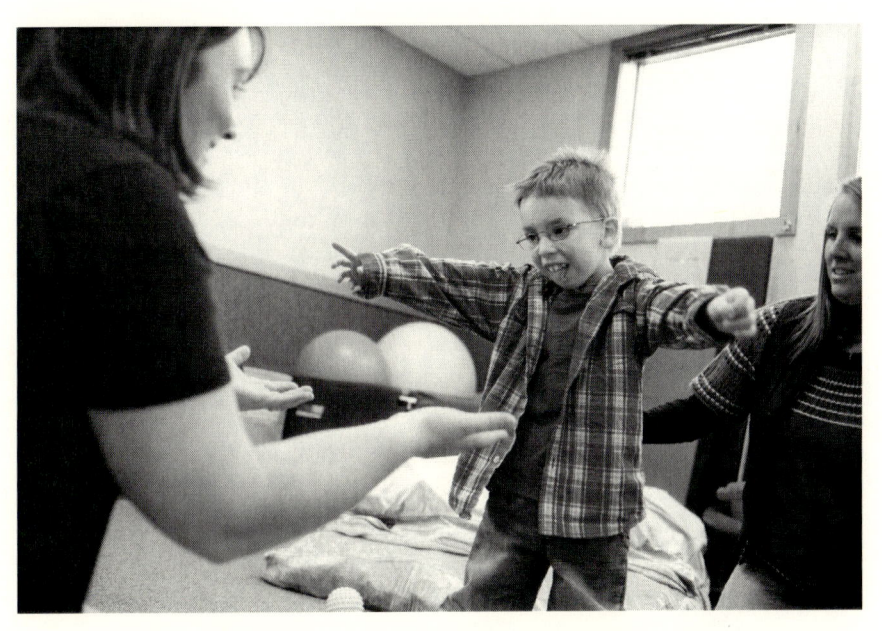

Ryder taking steps to his (PT) Therapist Karla Pezzarossi

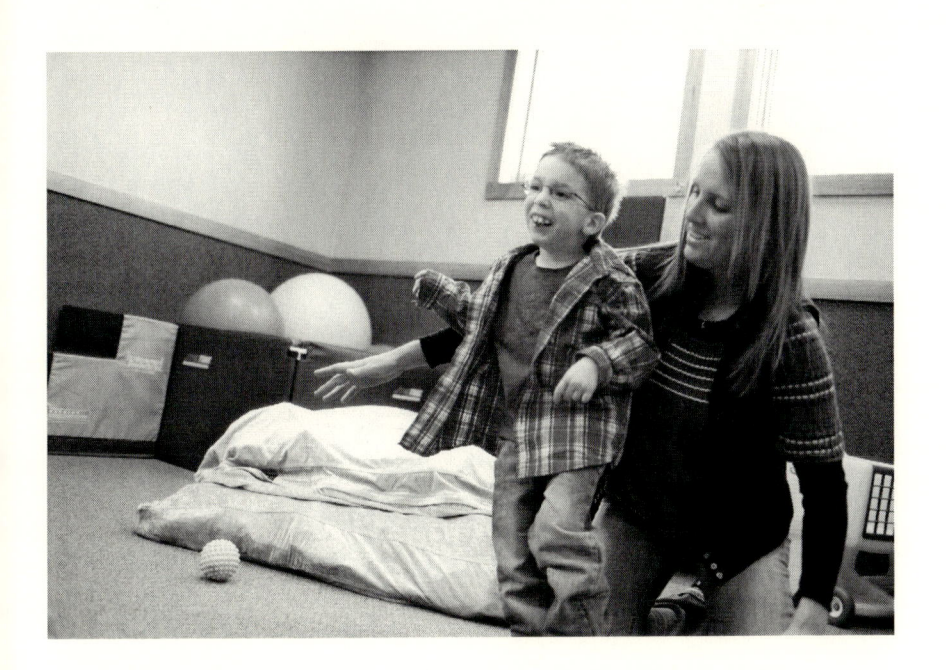

Ryder having more fun in PT working with Karla

Ryder and Therapist Azriel doing Medek

Ryder working hard in Medek

Ella with our Angel Colleen Roth "The Best OT",
Thank you for 6 great years!!!!!!

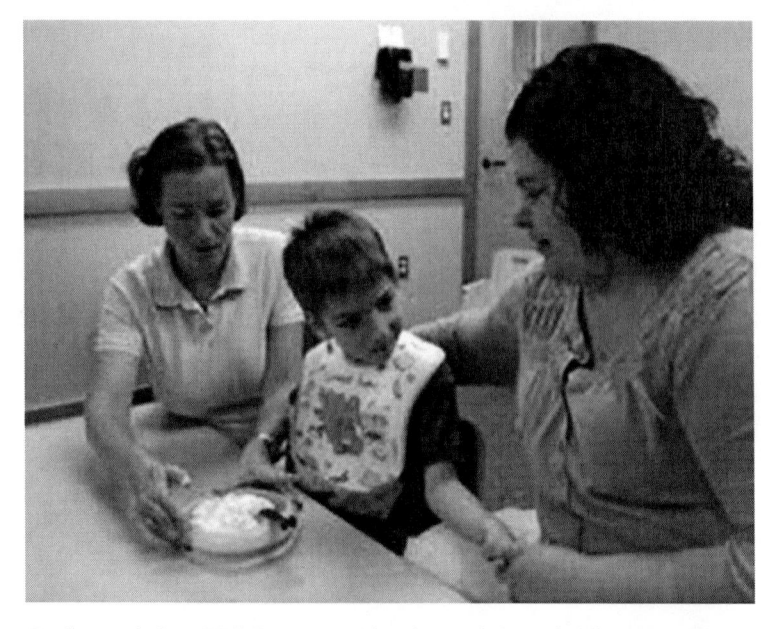

Ryder with his OT Therapist Claudia and Speech Therapist Marta

Chapter XI

Applied Behavioral Analysis (ABA)

Let's look at a little bit of history. In 1913, a psychologist named John Watson identified observable behavior as a proper subject matter for psychology. He felt that all behavior is controlled by events in the environment. Watson created a *stimulus response* that would become part of psychology. His research became part of the movement called *behaviorism*.

B. F. Skinner later clarified the distinction between Ivan Pavlov's *respondent conditioning* or conditioned reflexes (remember the dog and the bell?) and *operant conditioning*, in which the consequence of current behavior controls future behavior. Skinner outlined the basic principles of behavior that included reinforcement, prompting, fading, shaping, schedules, and rewarding. These principles comprise the pure science of behavior analysis. When these principles are taught and used, then it's called applied behavioral analysis (ABA). This means that the principles used to describe behavior are (1) observable, (2) lawful, and (3) measurable (got that?) and impact on the environment that surrounds the subject.

Ivar Lovaas (the main man) developed the idea further at UCLA in the 1960s. Lovaas began working on what later would be described as the *Me Book*. Others came along who created subcategories. Today we also have DTT, NET, and AVB. These are a curriculum of programs as well as teaching sequences that are used to teach them. These skills were taught as ABA. That means they teach using Lovaas's application of the science of behavioral analysis. AVB is the term applied to verbal behavior. It describes language in terms of its functions: intraverbals, tacts, mands. In order for your child to successfully master a skill, he should come in at 80 percent or more when measured in that specific area.

What does all this mean to you? Well, what child wouldn't do better with one-on-one instruction than with membership in a large group or class? ABA therapy is an extremely important teaching tool for all special-needs children precisely because it offers personal, rather than group, therapy. It breaks down even the smallest educational skill in order to acquire that skill and go from a specific setting to a general setting such as a large" Inclusion" classroom. In other words, it has been custom tailored to the needs of your specific child. Santosh and Ella have both spent fifteen hours a week in intensive ABA therapy since they were little, Santosh with discrete trials and Ella with some fluency training and floor time, as well as task analysis and discreet trial. Both children have blossomed in their cognitive learning skills using these approaches. With this type of therapy both children have also been successful in acquiring some of the physical information, like reflexes, they were born without.

Your family may have an apraxic child due to a number of umbrella conditions—i.e., global apraxia, autism, cerebral palsy, genetic diseases, and sensory-integration problems. Kids who have these disorders will suffer from attention-deficit and focus problems, both in the school and at home. Educationally, a child must have many tools in his belt in order to learn in a group environment. ABA is a type of therapy that helps a child cope with behavior issues, attending skills, and self-help skills.

ABA helps children reach their highest potential. It helps them overcome their attention disorders. It helps them control bad behavioral issues at home, in school, and in public!

Previously at home only in the world of autism, ABA is now entering the field of IEPs (personal records of an individual regarding test scores and relevant information), especially in public and private schools and clinics for special-needs children. ABA is now used for children with autism, and also for motor-impaired youngsters utilizing one-on-one teaching.

With ABA, a child repeats a task (or rep) over and over until it is learned. ABA teachers use task analysis and trials to teach many important, everyday tasks such as brushing teeth and getting dressed. Educational and academic skills are also taught such as categorizing, sorting, learning colors, and recognizing and counting numbers. Below is an interview with a primary source, an ABA teacher and therapist. She will answer some typical parent questions.

Q1) *How would you define ABA to a parent?* Applied behavioral analysis is a method of teaching that uses rewards to achieve a desired behavior. Repetition is used to ensure that the child learns and maintains the skill.

Q2) *What's so attractive about ABA therapy compared to a regular special-needs classroom setting with push-in models, and what are the basic fundamental differences?*

I like the structure of ABA therapy as well as the data collection and analysis. It's easy to look at a set of data and *determine quickly* and easily if the child is making progress or if a change needs to be made in programming. With ABA therapy, the child's program is entirely based on his or her unique needs. It is individualized and taught in a one-on-one or small group setting. This guarantees plenty of personal attention and the ability to continually assess a child's progress.

Q3) *What are the ages of the people you see?* One of my clients is five years old. Another is six.

Q4) *What made you want to work with the most severe cases of brain injuries?*

Working with children with disabilities is completely rewarding. It's a challenge on a daily basis, but the rewards are so much greater. When you experience success with a child with a disability, no matter how small, it's an amazing feeling. I love feeling that I am making a difference in that child's life—as well as in his family's.

Q5) *How many clients do you see in a day?*

I currently see two clients in a day.

Q6) *Do you feel there are enough of your ABA clinics to serve the population of kids properly?*

I feel that there are many wonderful schools, agencies, and therapists out there. However, some families do not seek out these people and places or are not financially or geographically able to seek out these quality services.

Q7) *How many school districts do you work with?* I currently work with one school district.

Q8) *What is your most amazing success story using ABA to date?*

Although there are many stories I could share, I am most proud to have worked with a boy who was declassified and no longer *has* a diagnosis. It's truly a testament to this wonderful boy and his team!

Q9) *With your experience working with people with traumatic brain injuries, what would be your advice for the parents who just found out about their child's diagnosis?*

From a purely professional standpoint, I can say they should educate themselves about various types of therapies, research schools, and agencies in their area. You are your child's best advocate, and your child will only benefit from your involvement in his or her education. Work closely with your child's teachers and therapists, and learn all that you can. This will help to improve your child's quality of life and that of your entire family.

Q10) *For those who are older and are just finding out about ABA, what would be your recommendation to help them receive services?*

Contact your local school district for information about what they provide. In New Jersey, the Division of Developmental Disabilities is another resource. Other states should have similar offices that can provide you with helpful information. There's also tons of information on the Internet to help you educate yourself. Parents can find support groups and connect with other parents of children with disabilities in their area to share information.

Q11) *Can you give us a short bio of your educational background?*

I began working with children with disabilities at a private school in New Jersey. As an aide there for about two and a half years, I learned and practiced principles of applied behavior analysis. I also began working on home programs, where I was able to learn even more working with talented coordinators. During this time, I earned my bachelor's degree and then taught a preschool disabled class in a public school district using applied behavior analysis. Following this, I taught for two years in a public school ABA program while working on a certificate in elementary education and another certificate as a teacher of students with disabilities. I was able to work with so many talented people in the field and gained much experience and knowledge. I currently work as a consultant for another school district, and I am also hired privately to shadow a student at his school.

Q12) *How does your family, and your community, feel about what your do? How has it impacted on your kids?*

My family is proud of me and is impressed by the work that I do. My husband definitely has respect for what I do. What I hear most when I tell people what I do is, "You must be so patient!"

Q13) *What type of materials is needed for a proper ABA program at home and at school?*

The materials will vary, based on the child's programming needs. Materials can include anything from a peer (to work on greetings), to a toothbrush and toothpaste, and from flash cards to objects found in a kitchen. It all depends on what goals are in the child's IEP, or what skills the student has the most trouble with, or are most important right now.

Q14) *How would I determine if ABA is right for my child?*

The child would be assessed in all skill areas, including receptive and expressive language and self-help skills. A set of programs can then be implemented. Should the child not show progress in a couple of weeks, changes can be made to the program. This might include a different teaching procedure or different materials. The wonderful part about ABA is that skills can be taught in so many different ways. If one method doesn't work, you can keep trying until you find success. In this way, ABA can help so many different children learn.

Q15) *In order for ABA to be successful for my child, how many hours a week would you say he would need?*

The number of hours per week will vary based on the child. For some students, five hours a week will be sufficient to progress in each goal. For others, even fifteen hours might not be enough. Each child has his or her own unique needs and situations, and all of these factors need to be taken into consideration when determining an appropriate amount of therapy time.

Q16) *What is the end goal of ABA?* The end goal of ABA is the learning of the desired behaviors. In short, ABA aims to help fulfill a child's goals.

End Interview

Parents, we strongly suggest that you call the local college near you, or a center for ABA, and ask for a screening. It's a science-based type of therapy and teaching procedure, which assesses behavior and then breaks it down to modify it a step at a time. This is called *task analysis*. While ABA is usually used with autism, the techniques have been proven to significantly help all children with developmental delays and other brain injuries.

This could be your plan: Take your child for an evaluation with a developmental pediatrician and psychologist. Get a letter and an evaluation that states that your child needs ABA therapy. Ask them for a minimum of fifteen hours of therapy a *week*. This letter and pre-evaluation cannot be ignored by your state. It will provide you with ABA therapy in your home, with a person who is licensed to work one-on-one with your child. *If* you demand it! This trained ABA therapist is a teacher who will take tasks and break them down into individual parts in order to work with them.

This therapy is one that is important. Its results are quantifiable and scientifically proven. The interaction of the environment around a child and the outside world is measurable. It uses a system of rewards to shape the undesirable current behavior into a more desired behavior. Through repetitions (called repeatability,) the therapist measures the number of times a child performs a task. It is then charted and repeated with consequences until the child obtains the adequate response or knowledge.

The cost: In parts of the United States and Canada, ABA is covered by Early Intervention and by the state, province, or Board of Education. However, if there is no coverage, there are private clinics available in most states that you can drive to, or you can enroll in an ABA program. The average session in the States is about $40 per hour.

Does insurance cover ABA? In most states, private insurance with proper documentation will cover your ABA hours if the diagnosis is autism. However, they don't tend to cover cerebral palsy and other traumatic brain injuries. In the new health-care bill in the USA, it is demanded that children with autism receive ABA hours at a low reimbursement rate; however, it states nothing about traumatic brain injuries or cerebral palsy.

To quote the New York State Department of Health and the State of Maine administrator of Services for Children of Disabilities, "stringently applied scientific standards of proof" have found that it alone, of all possible treatments for children with autism, has been proven effective. The panel members of many different agencies also second the overwhelming evidence that ABA has been proven highly effective for traumatic brain injuries and other brain injuries. Parents, we highly recommend this therapy. Research on behavior modification for brain-injured children and the designs of most studies show that the procedures used in behavioral modification work well with selected brain-injured children.

Lori: Seeing Ella do so well with ABA, I wish that I had known about ABA sooner for Ryder. Maybe then he would know such things as colors, shapes, and day-to-day tasks. But I know now, and I believe it's never too late to start. I hope by writing this book, other children can take advantage of the program at an earlier age. I'm angry that the Early Intervention Department and/or Ryder's neurologist in the state of Washington didn't present this ABA therapy to me at all. Ella currently receives ten hours of ABA a week in New Jersey and can recognize (read) several words.

Our advice to you on receiving ABA services: Get out there. Go! Fight! Win!

ABA Therapist, Kerry Fee

Ella wearing a PROTECTA CAP, working on holding a pencil in ABA age 3.5

Child Medium Walker

Chapter XII

Hyperbaric Oxygen Therapy (HBOT)

In the 1600s, humans used oxygen as a type of therapy to heal wounds. Who would have thought that, centuries later, we would still be using this therapy? Hyperbaric oxygen treatment (HBOT) has been used clinically since mid-1800s. The modern use of the HBOT was tested and developed by the US Military after WWI.

Hyperbaric oxygen therapy is a treatment meant to improve the body's natural healing process through the inhalation of 100 percent oxygen in a pressurized chamber. The *high chamber* is pressurized with ambient air to 1.75 ATA (1.75x normal atmospheric pressure). The patient breathes 100 percent pure oxygen through a special clear breathing hood or mask. Through this hood, the oxygen level is increased until it is many times above what is normal. According to one of the operators we spoke with, you go sixteen to eighteen feet below sea level. It's as if you are diving, and in fact each treatment is called a *dive*. It takes about twenty minutes to pressurize the tank, and at the end, another twenty minutes to come back up. A typical dive ranges from an hour and a half to an hour and forty-five minutes.

What is that supposed to accomplish? The purpose is to build new neurons and repair old damaged neurons in the areas of the brain. Oxygen has been known to help heal wounds such as fractures and other injuries like burns, scars, and even some organs to repair. This would certainly seem to include brain injuries caused by trauma after birth or oxygen deprivation *in utero*. Oh, by the way, we want to tell you that since we really aren't diving into water, there are no swim suits required!

There are several types of chambers:

Monoplace Chamber—According to the BaroMedical Research Centre, the monoplace chamber is the simplest and, most comfortable and effective chamber to use. It's designed for the single treatment of one person. With this type of chamber, the entire body can be immersed. The air pressure is two and a half to three times higher than the normal air pressure. The patient inhales pure oxygen from a hood or a mask placed on his head, and oxygen penetrates the body through the skin, which helps wash out the nitrogen from the body and saturate the organs with concentrated oxygen.

Topical Chamber—This is commonly used for a person who has a hard-to-heal or infected wound that is not responding to normal treatments. This type of chamber is disposable and comes in a box of four units, (a week's supply). It can be adjusted around parts of the body such as in a leg or an arm. According to the Wound Care Institute, the advantage of the topical chamber is that it can be used at home for the treatment of stubborn wounds. This allows the patient to remain in the comfort of his or her own home while receiving the treatment.

Multiplace Chamber—The air-compressed multiplace chamber offers oxygen therapy to treat anywhere from six to twelve individuals at one time and is considered less effective than the Monoplace Chamber. Again, for this treatment, bags are placed over each individual's head, which allows them to breath in the enhanced mixture of oxygen. In addition, within the chamber each person receives air pressure that is two and a half to three times higher than normal air pressure. This chamber can be more cost effective for medical centers to use, because of the increase in patients able to use the chamber at the same time. However, since this treatment is shared, it is not feasible to adjust the treatment to benefit any one individual.

Under normal circumstances, at sea level we breathe 21 percent oxygen along with smaller or larger amounts of other chemical gases. Red blood cells then funnel the oxygen to the various organs and muscles throughout the body. But if you can increase the amount of oxygen, you can direct it to the diseased or injured areas of the brain or body so that it can assist the body's natural defenses. White blood cells are the body's warriors against foreign invasion by viral and bacteriological infection. More oxygen means more reinforcement of white blood cells, and therefore, a more thorough job of protection. In the brain, new neurons are expected to be produced, which should repair old damaged cells or even supplement them. In many cases, such as in circulatory problems like nonhealing wounds and in strokes, adequate oxygen cannot reach the damaged area, and the body's natural healing ability is unable to function properly.

What are the side effects of such treatments? While there may be some discomfort to the ears (like the feeling you get on a plane when there is a sudden drop or rise of pressure) it usually dissipates. But once the pressure level has been reached, you feel much relief. Occasionally, people can get bad sinus infections. There are many ways to avoid this problem, like holding your nose and blowing out, sucking on candy, chewing many pieces of gum at a time, or drinking while you *dive*. Normally there's no pain or long-term discomfort at all. There may also be a worsening of nearsightedness (myopia) that typically disappears after about six weeks. Families have told us that vision actually has improved after this treatment. A few side effects we encountered were ear bleeds and burst eardrums, headaches and nausea. The majority of the children in this book have received over a hundred hours of HBOT and report nothing but positive results.

What we've seen researchers commonly note is that improvements in the parts of the cerebellum that control speech have been significantly improved. People with TBI and cerebral palsy, those who've suffered stroke, who are comatose, and others suffering brain impairments can be helped. We have seen the following improvements firsthand. We, together, have each completed two hundred dives. We have been in the chamber with a total of approximately twenty people between us. We'll tell you what we feel occurred with our own children.

Ryder was presented as a nonverbal, low-cognitive functioning child prior to his dives. There was a slight improvement in his decision-making skills; this seemed to be his only improvement thus far.

Ella was a CP hyperactive child with head tremors, which presents itself with constant head turning. She suffers from severe attention deficit disorder. After seventy-six dives, we noticed an increase in attending skills. Ella increased babbling; she also showed faster reaction times cognitively. It is hard to know what improvements Ella had from the HBOT directly, due to her participation in CE and stem cell therapy at that time. The women around me said, "she seems much quicker in response time to answering questions."

Sitting in the oxygen chamber with your kid may seem really scary. I was like, "She already had some anoxia. What if she suffocates more?" and "Is it safe?" During the two hundred or so dives we have taken with our kids, we discovered that one man had a grand mal seizure and two friends' sons also had seizures. Three strikes, right? But we learned that, if you have a predisposition to seizures, you are more likely to seize. So it's probably not a good idea if your child is prone to seizures.

But here's the good news! Three of the kids we went into the chamber with gained a tremendous increase in babbling, and were able to say a few words in the five weeks of HBOT.

Lou Brien has been at Ability Camp for fourteen years. He was a scuba driver who then decided to give what he knew, namely about increased air pressure, to children with developmental disabilities. He already knew that this was helpful improvements in muscle mobility in cases of stroke. Working with children with a variety of brain disorders, however, he noted a definite decrease in muscle tension. There are cognitive changes such as eye gaze and eye tracking improvements, and changes in speech. The possibility of growing healthy stem cells is also wonderful.

While centers around the world are demonstrating excellent results with this hyperbaric oxygen therapy, most doctors are not yet familiar with the basic laws of HBOT and consider the therapy very experimental. However, a growing number of doctors are utilizing this treatment on various different ailments much more frequently.

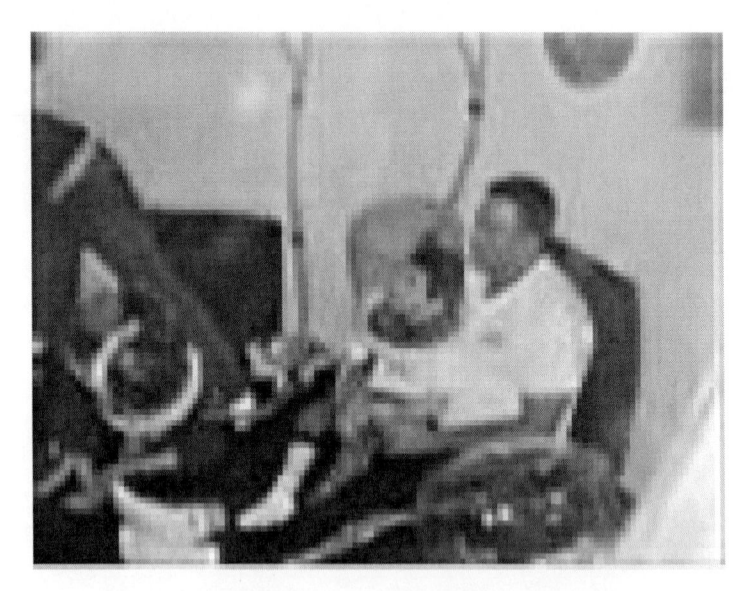

Cole and Dad Robert in the HBOT Chamber

Cole is the HBOT Chamber with his Mom Tiffany

Louis Brien, HBOT operator at the Ability Camp

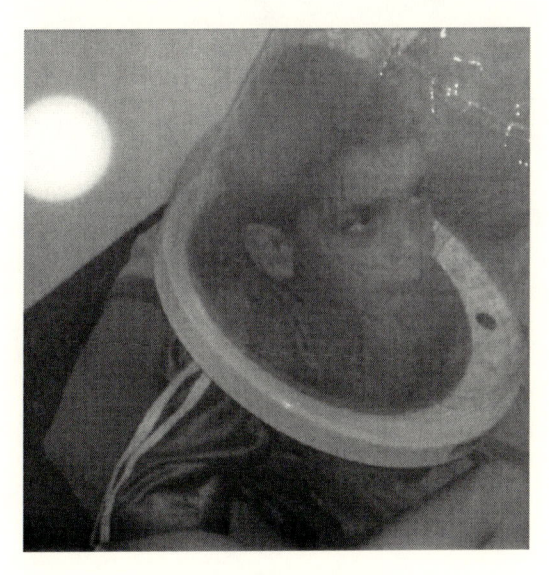

Ryder Hyperbarics

Chapter XIII

Stem Cell Replacement Therapy

There are two kinds of major stem cell implementations for TBI patients. The first is called autogeneous stem cell therapy. This may also be referred to as adult stem cell therapy. The second type could be considered very controversial, which is called embryonic stem cell replacement therapy.

In 2006, the United States began to allow the use of adult stem cells for the treatment of two diseases: leukemia and multiple sclerosis.

There are currently three ways to harvest and administer these stem cells: (1) take it from the patient's own body, (2) find a match from someone closely related to the patient, or (3) find a match from the donors registered with the federal government. But the match *must* be exact or there will be serious consequences to the patient's own body. If your body is not prepared to accept the new cells and the procedure is not done perfectly, it can turn around and attack the host's cells.

While various laboratories around the world began to experiment with stem cells, one or two particular labs, one (the X-Cell Center in Dusseldorf) in Germany and another in China began to study an approach that used the host's own stem cell for the replacement. For this autogeneous approach, the lab extracts stem cells from the blood harvested with a lumbar puncture (lower spine) or spinal tap. To greatly simplify, eight to twelve vials of bone marrow, containing blood and undifferentiated stem cells, are withdrawn from the hip area of the child or adult via a spinal tap. In Ella's case, she was under anesthesia. The process takes about fifteen minutes. The stem cells are separated from the mixture, placed under a microscope, purified, and reintroduced by injection to the upper spinal area near the neck, or even into the brain. It seems that the pelvic area of the body contains a number of undifferentiated cells. These new, healthy cells will replace some of the brain cells that were damaged, whether traumatically or in utero.

My daughter Ella and I went on our first journey for autogeneous stem cell replacement in 2009. The idea of going to Dusseldorf was both exciting and scary the first time. But once you've gone through the travel, and your child has had the procedure, it really isn't as bad as it sounds. The time needed in Germany amounts to five or six days. Once her cells were harvested, Ella's body began to produce new ones in preparation for another round next year.

We have gone twice. The first time, we noticed a significant improvement in her cognitive developmental function. She appeared BRIGHTER in understanding two step and three step commands. She was able to lift her hands over her head for the first time, and also moving a cup from one side to another. Ella's CP hands, usually closed into a fist, completely opened. I could actually see her fingernails anytime I wanted to! In the past year after the procedure we have seen only a slight regression in her improvements except in cognitive developments. The second visit worked on her oral motor area, which has been so hard to deal with. Now she can open her mouth and brush her teeth. We are hopeful that now, at five, she will learn to chew her food and perhaps say more than three or four words.

The child or adult who uses his or her own stem cells will have no rejection problems. There may be an intense headache for a day or two following replacement, but there will be a 7 percent to 20 percent increase in the functioning of some part of the brain, whether it's in a physical realm, or in speech and receptive language, or in the area of cognizance.

Although I loved seeing Dusseldorf, a beautiful city, there's no reason that my own country could not foster the proper environment for more advanced stem cell research and development. If the patient is willing to take the risk (the risk of a lumbar puncture going wrong is very low), the procedure would become available to so many more children. Why is it that they are willing to do a lumbar puncture procedure on multiple sclerosis and cancer patients but not for children with cerebral palsy, especially if they are willing to take the risk? It would cut costs dramatically if parents could stay in their own country instead of having to fly halfway across the world. I'm sure that it's just a matter of time before stem cell replacement therapy becomes a nearly routine procedure, but for a special-needs child, time is running out.

In case you're wondering, a stem cell treatment costs about ten thousand American dollars. As we go to the press, our Ella will have had two stem cell transfusions, both with really great results. Since the stem cell treatment, she has really responded to her other therapies at a hugely increased rate. All we have is anecdotal evidence to support the benefits of stem cells, but the families we have stayed in contact with, from Sydney to London to Tel-Aviv, have all reported similar findings. Unhappily, recent news from Germany is that the X-Cell Center in Dusseldorf has closed. It's only a matter of time, however, before some other lab opens to replace it.

Our OT Jennifer Ingelett came over with us to research firsthand the benefits of stem cell therapy. Jennifer runs a suit therapy workshop in New Jersey and is very aggressive and interactive with impaired children.

She videotaped Ella's walking and play skills prior to the second stem cell procedure. She videotaped throughout the week of Ella's stem cell procedure. Also, she videotaped Ella one week and two weeks after. She wrote an article on her observations for the American Physical Therapy Association.

Cole Hicks (Rocky) has also attended the X-Cell Center with remarkable results in his overall cognitive receptive skills and stronger muscle tone in his core. However, since we began the writing of this book, unfortunately, there were two incidents at the center that both came from a procedure whereby they placed the stem cells directly through the brain into the cerebral cortex. The lead pediatric neurosurgeon was under investigation and, unfortunately, the German government has currently placed a halt on all stem cell procedures at the X-Cell Center.

We acknowledge that there are other locations that are popular for stem cell therapy such as the Bieke Institute in China and the Institute for Regenerative Medicine stem cell therapy located in Arizona. In addition, there are procedures in stem cell therapy in California/Tijuiana with Dr. Steenblock. Again, we are looking to explore the benefits of autogenous stem cells firsthand with our children prior to endorsing these other places. We have heard of some success in Costa Rica as well.

By now, I'm sure you have read the websites on cerebral palsy that explained how it was caused by a traumatic brain injury of some kind, and have noted the different types of CP that your child could have. To understand a disease or a lifelong condition, you have to be knowledgeable about the subject area. I would tell you to spend as much time researching CP and following assertive technologies and assertive therapy for it as you possibly can. You would spend hours training a puppy to go outside. You would spend hours researching a term paper for a college course. Well, this is your child.

Outlook and Advice

There is nothing more precious, nothing more important than to gain knowledge and become an expert on your child's lifelong condition. Prepare yourself to become a parent advocate, prepare yourself to be a fighter, and above all, have an optimistic outlook that things will and can get better. We are only mothers with children who have severe disabilities, but we can all testify to the fact that each of our children has far exceeded what we were told by doctors would be our child's limitations in life. If you can learn anything from this book, it's that there is a cocktail for living with cerebral palsy in a successful manner.

We want to share with you the impact these special children bring to the whole family. If you have other children, it is very important to make them feel wanted and loved. And never forget they may feel like there's upheaval and that Mommy and Daddy are sad for some reason.

I can share with you what we did with our own daughters. We make sure that there was always someone at home with them, and that their lives were disrupted as little as possible. They were enrolled in after-school activities. We also hired a sleep-in nanny who came to love our girls, but who became absolutely devoted to Ella.

Mommy and Ella Day Four of Stem Cells in Germany

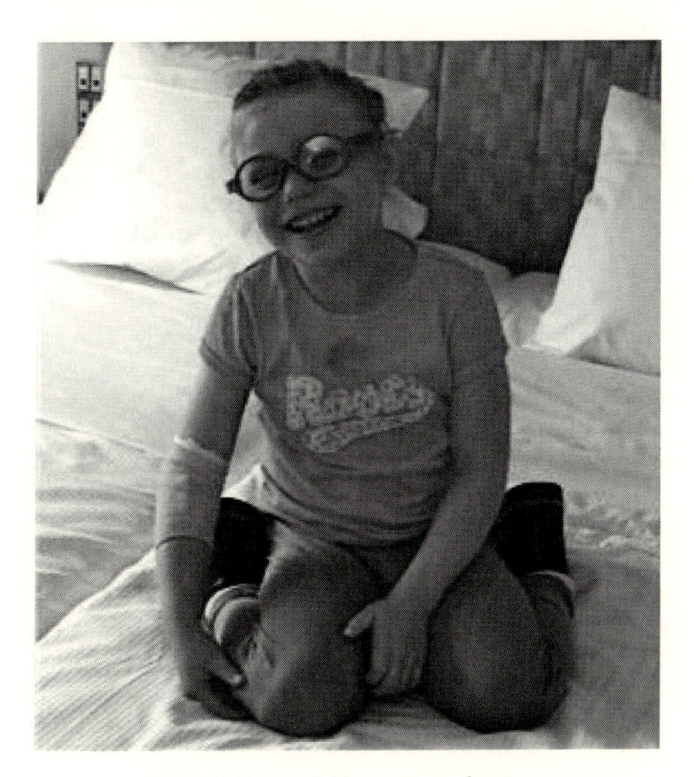

X-Cell Center Ella on Transfer Day

Ella taking steps out of her chair in Dusseldurf, Germany

Miss Jenn Inglit and EllaBella in Germany for Stem-cells!
We saw a difference!

Chapter XIV

Deal with IEP and Your School District

First, let us tell you what an IEP is. We sure didn't know much, and we certainly didn't know our rights. We learned quickly. With better knowledge and with a renewed perseverance to better care for our children, we learned how to fight to get what our children need, being as aggressive as possible.

We have both learned so much on our journey that we opened businesses as advocates, Tamara on the East Coast *(www.eastcoastspecialneedsadvocate.org)* and Lori on the West Coast. Here are the main rules used when working through the IEP process.

Number one: try to lay out your wants, hopes, and individual goals on paper. The district will have its own idea of how to educate your kids, but unfortunately, it is within the mold of minimal education, typically not adequate and not appropriate. No school district can come out and say, "It costs way too much to follow an educational plan that would be truly appropriate and adequate." (With more money spent, the child would reach desired goals more quickly, but this doesn't happen in reality.)

Children with any type of brain injury, genetic disorder, or cognitive delay all learn best through intensive, repetitious, consistent, and aggressive therapies. These *cost money!* Districts are naturally at odds with a family asking for five days a week of PT, five days of OT, five days of speech therapy, ABA, ABM, augmentative communication hours, Visual therapy, and Assistive Technology hours until there is proficiency. Just think, if they gave those hours to all children who were mildly to significantly delayed, the district would go broke. In conjunction with an advocate and possibly a special-needs attorney, families with special-needs children will almost always increase their placement, hours of service, and the expertise level of practitioners assigned to work with their children. Unfortunately, this comes at a huge cost, both financially and emotionally, to the families of special-needs children.

We will begin with a quick definition of the individualized education program (IEP). An IEP describes the educational plan that has been designed to meet a specific child's unique needs. The IEP creates an opportunity for teachers, parents, school administrators, related services personnel, and students (when age appropriate) to work together to improve results for children with disabilities. The IEP is the cornerstone of a quality education for each child. It makes it possible to progress toward meeting annual goals and objectives. The IEP includes any assistance and accommodation necessary to arrive at these goals. It offers periodic reports and ongoing data on progress or lack thereof. It discusses inclusion and transition services over summer, weekends, holidays, etc. This is referred to as ESY or extended school year.

Parents: Here's a very important list of individualized accommodations that can be put into place to help your child have success in academic programs or IEP.

*Ability Grouping—A few peers who work with your child's weaknesses to help him.
*Graphic organizers (charts, graphs, etc.)
*Time management skills
*Provide a buddy
*Provide assistive technology and training and augmentative communication
*Larger font size
*Special materials for the visually impaired
*A one-to-one aide

Note: The individualized education program (IEP) is a legally binding document. It establishes a plan for an individual who meets the following eligibility criteria: he child is identified as having one or more of thirteen classified disabilities. You can count sensory as one or as three separate disabilities: hearing, vision, deaf-blind defined in state and federal laws. The state's definition of special ed disabilities: autism, pervasive developmental disorders (PDD, PDD/NOS), Asperger's disorder, Rett's disorder, childhood disintegrative disorder (CDD), developmentally delayed, and emotional impairment.

The federal government also uses terms like *emotional disturbance,* which includes pervasive moods of unhappiness or depression or a tendency to develop physical symptoms or fears associated with personal or school problems over a long period. Note that naming a type of disability isn't the same as making a diagnosis. It's a more general agreement among team members that the assessed characteristics of the student comply with the regulatory definition for that type of disability(ies). In other words, the definitions are general definitions. Each one comprises many subgroups, with specific associated diagnostic criteria which are often medical in nature.

It's not the intention of the special education law to require a specific diagnosis such as *Asperger's syndrome* or *cerebral palsy*. Medical personnel use criteria that include educational impact as only one aspect of the diagnostic process, and they will generally only provide those specific diagnoses.

But special education eligibility is both more specific and more general. The use of the disability label is more general, but the consideration of educational impact is very specific. Some of the assessors who provide information to the team may be in a position to make a medical diagnosis, and the diagnosis may, therefore, be a part of the team discussion. However, although a team may use a diagnosis made available to it as part of the assessment information, it's not the responsibility of the team to either confirm or deny a diagnosis made by an assessor.

Teams should not spend time, therefore, attempting to agree on an exact diagnosis, as long as the assessment information is sufficient to make the more general assertion that the student has a certain type of disability. Conversely, teams may often have conflicting information provided by assessors, including medical professionals, who have made a diagnosis naming a specific disability or disorder. Teams are not obligated to resolve such conflicts or to accept such diagnoses as sufficient to require the provision of special education services. In fact, the special education law explicitly requires that a team of people, including educators and the child's parent(s), make a determination of eligibility. Although medical personnel may be members of a team, they cannot be the only voice, since the determination of eligibility for special education is an educational, not a medical, decision.

Is your son or daughter able to progress effectively in regular education despite his/her disability? To *progress effectively* means to make documented growth in the acquisition of knowledge and skills, which includes social and emotional development in the general education program. There are chronological age and developmental exceptions. The individual educational potential of the child must also be taken into consideration.

Massachusetts C online copy of the Reign. The following statements are from the IEP Process Guide by the Massachusetts Department of Education/ June 2001.

"Teams sometime struggle in trying to decide if a student is making effective progress and look for specific guidelines to assist in making this important decision. Effective progress, however, is not easily translated to test scores, academic achievement, social skills, or other individual or specific variables, but rather is an interrelated measure.

Teams, therefore, should carefully review evaluation data and make student-centered decisions on this important issue."

The Department of Education has a flowchart to be used in a team meeting as an aid for determining if your child meets the criteria of the two questions asked above. It's called the *special education eligibility determination form.*

Here's a quick definition of IDEA 2004 (The Individuals with Disabilities Education Act):

IDEA is the federal law that secures special education services for children with disabilities from the time they're born 'til they graduate from high school.

This law was reauthorized by Congress in 2004, prompting a series of changes in the way special ed services are implemented. These changes are continuing today and they affect the delivery of special education and related services in your state. The IDEA Partnership can help you keep up with the changes and possibly influence future decisions.

What happens if my child is not found to be eligible?

"If your child is not found eligible, you may still receive help, although not special education services. If your child is not eligible for special education services, you will receive a letter from the school stating that your child is not eligible, detailing why the student was found not eligible, along with information about your rights. Read the notice carefully to decide if you agree or disagree with this decision. You have the right to appeal a "finding of no eligibility." You might also ask for an IRNS meeting within your school, or a 504 plan for your child.

The above statement is from *A Parent's Guide to Special Education*, which is a joint publication of the Federation for Children with Special Needs and the Massachusetts Department of Education. Parents can reject the *finding of no eligibility* and request an independent evaluation (IEE) or use their insurance to cover the cost of IEE. Parents can also request a redetermination of eligibility based on new information for the team to consider.

The following statements are from *IEP Process Guide* by the Massachusetts Department of Education (June 2001).

"The Parent also has the right to appeal any eligibility determination to the Bureau of Special Education Appeals, including a finding of no eligibility. Parent may contact the bureau directly or request district assistance in contacting this agency.

Parent should be asked if they agree with the evaluation findings.

"Team members should check a parent's understanding of the evaluation data and their agreement with it. If the parent disagrees with a particular school assessment, parents may have a right to an independent evaluation (IEE)."

Hey, parents, there is a chance that your child is actually not qualified. However, if your child is like the children in this book, you will need an IEP. A student is not eligible if the team determines that to be the case. The team chairperson records the reason, lists the meeting's participants, and provides written notice to the parents of their rights in accordance with the federal requirements within ten (10) days of the team meeting. If your child had an IEP and now is deemed no longer eligible, you can reject the finding and request a hearing, and your child's IEP will remain in effect until the hearing officer makes a decision.

The team reconsiders eligibility when a student is reevaluated. When a student is referred for a reevaluation, the school district should first review existing evaluation data. If no additional information is needed to determine whether the student continues to be eligible, the school district may request that a parent waive particular types of assessment(s). The parent may either consent to waive the assessment(s) or may choose to have the assessment completed regardless of the recommendation for waiver.

At the reevaluation team meeting, the team, after determining the existence of a disability(ies), must decide whether the student would continue to make progress in school without the continued provision of special education services. A student's progress should not be judged solely on the completion of IEP goals or report card grades. It requires that the student be evaluated before determining that the child is no longer eligible.

FEDERAL LAW, Section 614 of the Individuals with Disabilities Education Act, IDEA (20 U.S.C. 1414) reads as follows:

> Evaluations before change in eligibility—a local educational agency shall evaluate a child with a disability in accordance with this section before determining that the child is no longer a child with a disability.

Students between ages of three to twenty-one are eligible for an IEP.

(Children who are ages zero to three are eligible for individual family service plan [IFSP]).

- The following is a summary of what is contained in the IEP:
- The student's disability(ies)
- A vision statement of the student's long-term goal (one to five years in the future)
- Describe how the student's disability(ies) affects his progress in the classroom
- Short-term goals based upon the child's own learning strengths and weaknesses
- How the child's progress toward these goals will be measured and how will the goals be evaluated
- Accommodations and modifications
- For students with behavioral or emotional issues that interfere with their learning, the IEP should contain a program designed to teach the student appropriate behavior and social skills. All behavior management techniques are to be used
- Summer services
- Transportation needs
- Type of placement.

IEP References:

Federation for Children with Special Needs, IEP for My Child.

IEP Process Guide (June 2001) is a manual that was created by the DOE that describes each page of the IEP. You can call and order your own copy of this guide, DOE (781) 338-6203. Publication by DOE Special Education Policy and Planning Department x3375.

Continuum of Options for Dispute Resolution

(1) **Local School District Procedures.** School districts are encouraged to develop local problem resolution procedures that allow parents to present a concern to a district representative and receive a response related to the concern. Local procedures shall not be used to delay or deny a parent's right to access other dispute resolution mechanisms.

(2) **Department Procedures.** The Department maintains a Problem Resolution System that provides for the investigation of complaints and the enforcement of compliance. Other statutes and regulations relating to the provision of publicly funded education. The Department can make findings on procedural issues and issues related to implementation of requirements. Any party wishing to file a complaint may do so through the Department. Use of the Department Problem Resolution procedures shall not prevent a party from requesting alternative administrative remedies of mediation or hearing on any matter, at any time. Copies of the Problem Resolution System Guidelines and Procedures are available from the Department upon request. Findings and orders issued by the Department on complaints and the Department's processing of a complaint are not reviewable by the Bureau of Special Education Appeals. Additionally, the pendency of a complaint before the Department does not make the Department a necessary party to actions on related issues pending before the Bureau of Special Education Appeals.

(3) **Bureau of Special Education Appeals: Jurisdiction.** In order to provide for the resolution of differences of opinion among school districts, private schools, parents, and state agencies, the Bureau of

Special Education Appeals, located with the Department, shall conduct mediations and hearings to resolve such disputes. The jurisdiction of the Bureau of Special Education Appeals over state agencies, however, shall be exercised consistent with 34 CFR §300.154(a). The hearing officer may determine, in accordance with the rules, regulations and policies of the respective agencies, that services shall be provided by the Department of Social Services, the Department of Mental Retardation, The Department of Mental Health, the Department of Public Health, or any other state agency or program, in addition to the IEP services to be provided by the school district. Mediations and hearings shall be conducted by impartial mediators and hearing officers who do not have personal or professional interests that would conflict with their objectivity in the hearing or mediation and who are employed to conduct those proceedings.

(a) A parent or a school district, may request mediation and/or a hearing at any time on any matter concerning the eligibility, evaluation, placement, IEP, provision of special education in accordance with state and federal law, or procedural protections of state and federal law for students with disabilities. A parent of a student with a disability may also request a hearing on any issue involving the denial of the free appropriate public education guaranteed by Section 504 of the Rehabilitation Act of 1973.

(b) No later than five days after receipt of a request for hearing or notice that the parent has rejected an IEP, or proposed placement, or finding of no eligibility for special education, the school district shall send a copy of such request or notice to the Bureau of Special Education Appeals. The Bureau of Special Education Appeals shall then give notice in writing to the parties of the rights of the parents and school district to request mediation and a hearing.

(c) A school district may not request a hearing on a parent's failure or refusal to consent to initial evaluation or initial placement of a student in a special education program.

(d) A school district may request a hearing to appeal the Department's assignment of school district responsibility under 603 CMR 28.10

(4) **Mediation.** A voluntary dispute resolution procedure, called mediation, shall be provided by mediators employed by the Bureau of Special Education Appeals and may be used by parents and school districts to seek resolution of their dispute. Mediations shall be provided at no cost to the parties. No parent shall be required to participate in mediation.

 (a) Within thirty (30) days of receipt of a request for mediation, the mediator shall schedule a mediation session at a time and place convenient to the parties. The mediation shall include the parents, any representative of the parents' choosing, and a representative(s) of the school district, with one representative who is authorized to resolve the dispute on behalf of the school district. When the parties reach agreement, it shall be set forth in written form. Concurrent with a request for mediation or if no agreement is reached, the parents or school district may request a hearing.

 (b) All discussions that occur during mediation are confidential and may not be used as evidence in a hearing. Parents and school districts may request a hearing without participating in mediation.

(5) **Hearings.** Five (5) days after receipt of a written request for hearing, the Bureau of Special Education Appeals shall notify the parties in writing of the name of the assigned hearing officer and, as appropriate, shall provide either a date for the hearing or a statement of federally required procedures to be followed before a hearing date can be assigned.

 (a) The Bureau of Special Education Appeals shall issue Rules that state the parties' rights and obligations as to the hearing process, which shall be consistent with all state and federal laws. Such Rules shall be available to the public on request.

 (b) Except as provided otherwise under federal law or in the administrative rules adopted by the Bureau of Special Education Appeals, hearings shall be conducted consistent with the formal Rules of Administrative Procedures.

(c) The Special Education Appeals hearing officer shall have the power and the duty to conduct a fair hearing; to ensure that the rights of all parties are protected; to define issues; to receive and consider all relevant and reliable evidence; to ensure an orderly presentation of the evidence and issues; to order additional evaluations by the school district or independent education evaluations at public expense when necessary in order to determine the appropriate special education for the student; to reconvene the hearing at any time prior to the issuance of a decision; to take such other steps as are appropriate to assure the orderly presentation of evidence and protection of the parties' rights at the hearing; to ensure a record is made of the proceedings; and to reach a fair, independent, and impartial decision based on the issues and evidence presented at the hearing and in accordance with applicable law.

(6) **Hearing Decision.** The decision of the hearing officer of the Bureau of Special Education Appeals shall be implemented immediately and shall not be subject to reconsideration by the Bureau of Special Education Appeals or the Department, but may be appealed to a court of competent jurisdiction.

(a) The written findings of fact and decision of the hearing officer along with notification of the procedures to be followed with respect to appeal and enforcement of the decision shall be sent to the parties and their representatives.

(b) A party contending that a Bureau of Special Education Appeals decision is not being implemented may file a motion with the Bureau of Special Education Appeals contending that the decision is not being implemented and setting out the areas of non-compliance. The hearing officer may convene a hearing at which the scope of the inquiry shall be limited to the facts on the issue of compliance, facts of such a nature as to excuse performance, and facts bearing on a remedy. Upon a finding of non-compliance, the hearing officer may fashion appropriate relief, including referral of the matter to the Legal Office of the Department or other office for appropriate enforcement action. The possibility of enforcement action does not make the Department a necessary party in matters pending before the Bureau of Special Education Appeals.

(7) **Student's right to IEP services and placement.** In accordance with state and federal law, during the pendency of any dispute regarding placement or services, the eligible student shall remain in his or her then current education program and placement unless the parents and the school district agree otherwise.

(a) If the parents are seeking initial placement in the public school, and the child is at least five years old, however, the child shall be placed in the public school program.

(b) For children three and four years of age, rights to services from the public school district are limited to children who have been found eligible for special education and have an IEP and placement proposed by the public school district and accepted by the parent.

(c) A hearing officer may order a temporary change in placement of an eligible student for reasons consistent with federal law, including but not limited to when maintaining such student in the current placement is substantially likely to result in injury to the student or others.

(d) Any party seeking to change the eligible student's placement during the pendency of proceedings before the Bureau of Special Education Appeals or in subsequent judicial proceedings shall seek a preliminary injunction from a state or federal court of competent jurisdiction, ordering such a change in placement.

In the long run, if you put in the time NOW to educate yourself about your rights, and state and federal educational laws, it will vastly aid your special-needs child and your family as a whole. Every day makes a difference!

Parents, I want to share that I have learned that the best "Advocate" for one's child is one who works within the system and slowly changes systems from with-in. In the long run it is very benificial to establish a good working relationship with your child's school district. I am proud of the work Dr. Faye Brady in Warren Twp. NJ has done with me on Ella's Program, Placement, and Services. We are both learning each and everyday what is effective and what isn't.

185

Adaptive Strollers can be covered by DDD or Private Insurance!

Ella and Lexi Kindergarten Graduation

IEP session

School and your IEP teachers

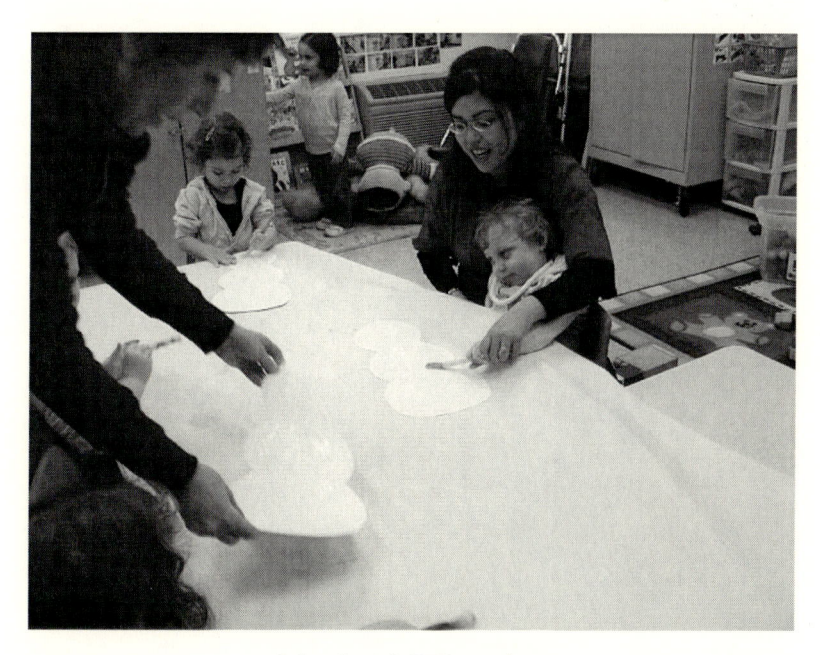

School with IEP teachers

Kindergarten at Mt. Horeb School

Ryder and his favorite Teacher Mrs. Hilyard

Ryder loves school

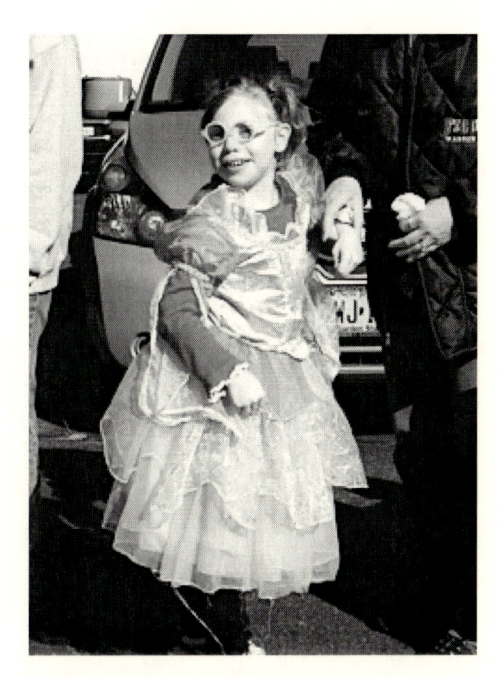

Halloween Parade 2011

Halloween 2011 Ella and Miss Mary

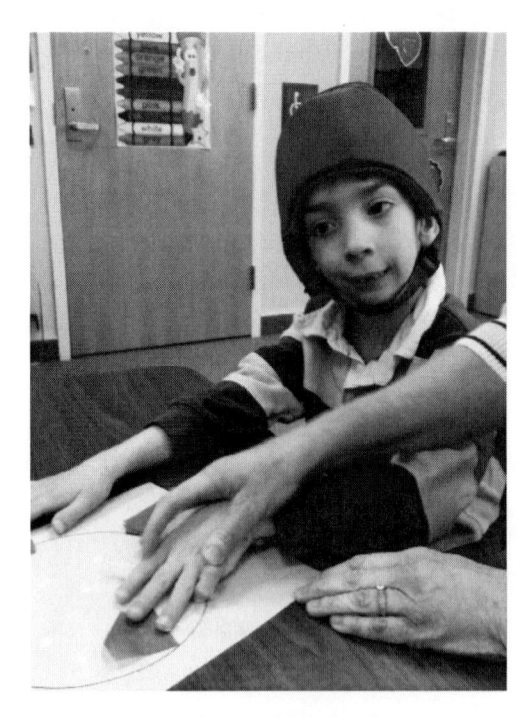

Ryder working hard

Ryder bowling in Physical Ed class

Ryder making a snowman at school

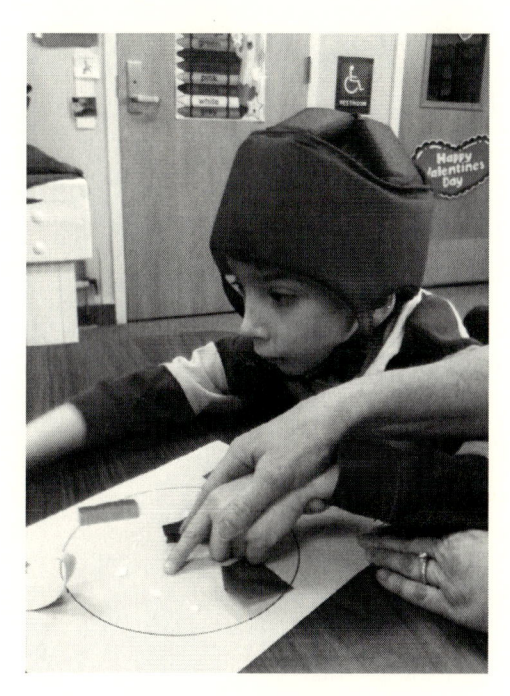

Ryder at school

Part IV
Conclusion

Since we started this book our two children, Ella and Ryder, as well as the other children discussed in this book, have made significant progress. Ryder and Ella have since gained skills in communication, cognizance, language and balance.

Lori brought Ryder twice to New Jersey for Medek. He has shown improvement in his core and in his balance. He is physically doing well. He has since given up some of his wall-walking, and now takes many steps independently in the hall. Ryder has also taken four trips to Ability Camp, where he improved in physical balance, decision—making and behavioral skills.

With Ella's two stem cell transplants in Germany, we saw a huge change in her comprehension and the rapidity with which she responds to conversation and command. We heard that other children were using Botox, and tried it. She has now done Botox and had good gains in dealing with the rounding of her back. Our three trips up to Ability Camp in Ontario have resulted in increased babbling, a precursor of speech, and many daily life skills. She achieved a 50 percent success rate in potty training. She can self-feed with prompting and is using her hands much more.

Our journeys have been long and hard-fought, but we know that although they will change over time, they will never really end. We hope that what we have experienced with our children, and the knowledge we have shared with you in this book, will help you develop your own cocktail for success. Yes, your life will be different, but these special children have so much to offer and will enrich the life of you and your family so much that you'll agree: your life is just a *"different kind of wonderful."*

Index

A

ABA (applied behavior analysis), 73–74, 151–57, 174
Ability Camp, 19–21, 62–63, 73, 130–32, 163, 193
Adeli suit. *See* TheraSuit
Adivan, 19
AFOs, 60–62, 71
American Physical Therapy Association, 169
aphasia, 28
apraxia, 61, 82–83, 122, 137, 152, 202
aqua therapy, 140
Asperger's disorder, 175
autism, 26, 72, 77–78, 80, 152, 156–57, 175
Ayurveda (Indian massage), 71

B

Baclofen, 19
barium swallow study, 31
BaroMedical Research Centre, 161
Bateman, Christopher, 80
Benik Vest, 60–61
Be Rachel's Miracle (fundraising event), 62–63
bilirubin, 27
Biondi, Peter, 79
Bonner, Michael, 55–58, 60–61
Bonner, Rachel, 55, 57–64
Bonner, Ross, 55
Bonner, Seth, 55
Bonner, Tina, 55–63
Bo Ra. *See* Bonner, Rachel
Botox, 45–46, 60, 193
Brenda (Ability Camp instructor), 130
Bureau of Special Education Appeals, 177, 180–84

C

Cargan, Abba, 28
cataracts, 68
Catherine (Wyatt's personal aide), 27, 91

CAT scan (computerized axial tomography), 28, 89
CDD (childhood disintegrative disorder), 175
CE (conductive education), 20, 48, 119, 128–32, 163
cerebral palsy (*see also* CP), 26, 28–29, 33, 45, 90, 120–21, 124, 128–29, 137–38, 152, 157, 162, 168–70, 175, 202
cleft palate, 42–43, 122
CME therapy, 135–37, 140. *See also* Medek
Colleen (occupational therapist), 28
Columbia Presbyterian Hospital, 77
Cotton, Ester, 129–30
CP (*see also* cerebral palsy), 32–33, 55, 57, 59, 62, 128, 138–39, 163, 167, 169
CPAP (continuous positive airway pressure), 87
Cuevas, Ramon, 135
CVS (chorionic villus sampling), 67

D

Dana (speech therapist), 28
David (Marykate's father), 76
D&C (dilation and curettage), 25
Debbie (Tina Bonner's sister), 55, 61–62
Diestat, 72
diparesis, 89
Disability Awareness Day, 79
Division of Developmental Disabilities, 154
DuPont, 80
dysphasia, 28, 122
dystonia, 83

E

Early Intervention, 30–31, 157
eczema, 70–71
EEG (electroencephalogram), 72, 89
ELISA testing, 74
Ella, 24, 27–33, 130, 136, 139, 152, 157, 163, 167–70, 193, 202
EmPower Somerset, 78
EpiPen, 71
Erikson, Erik, 120
ESY (extended school year), 78, 174

F

failure to thrive, 122
Federation for Children with Special Needs, 177
feeding therapy, 119
Ferrera, Anthony, 79
First World Congress on Conductive Education, 129
Fruits of the Spirit, 56

G

GAPS diet, 74
genetic testing, 50, 89
GERD (gastroesophageal reflux disease), 29–30, 89, 122–23
G-tube (gastrostomy), 28–30, 32, 45–46, 122, 124

H

Hari, James, 128
Hari, Maria, 129

HBOT (hyperbaric oxygen treatment), 19, 74, 160, 162–63
  types
    monoplace chamber, 161
    multiplace chamber, 161
    topical chamber, 161
Heal, Laird, 128
Hickling, Kevin, 130
Hicks, Austin, 13, 16
Hicks, Briana, 13, 16
Hicks, Cole "Rocky," 13–21, 136, 169
Hicks, Robert, 13, 15–19, 80
Hicks, Tiffany, 13
hippotherapy, 74, 140
homeopathic medicine, 59
House (professor)***, 128
hydrocephaly, 122
hypertonia, 28, 122
hypotonia, 28, 45, 81, 122

I

IACEA (Inter-American Conductive Education Association), 130
IEP (individualized education program), 78, 152, 155, 173–79, 181, 184
IKEA, 131
IMC project, 128
Infant Development Services, 69
Ingelett, Jennifer, 139, 168
Institute for Human Potential, 70
Institute for Regenerative Medicine, 169
International College of Pediatrics, 129
IRSE, 78
IUI (artificial insemination), 25

J

Jacobson, Alan, 27, 31, 202
Jacobson, Alexandra Rose. *See* Lexi
Jacobson, Elizabeth Catherine. *See* Ella
Jacobson, Laura, 25–27, 29–30, 32, 202
Jacobson, Tamara Lee, 173, 201
jaundice, 27–28, 67, 122

K

Kate (Wyatt's physical therapist), 91
Kaye reverse walker, 60
Kayleigh***, 76–77
Kingsbrook Jewish Medical Center, 129
Kmart, 131
Koscielny, Isabella, 138
Koscielny, Richard, 138
Kristina (Ability Camp instructor), 130

L

laparoscopic surgery, 25
Lenox Hill Hospital, 76
Lexi, 27, 29–30, 32, 202
Lisa (physical therapist), 59
Lovaas, Ivar, 151
LRE (least restrictive environment), 78
Lucas, Jerry, 129

M

Marykate***, 75–77, 79–80
Massachusetts Department of Education, 176–77
Matheny School, 130

McAuley School, 79
meconium aspiration syndrome, 56
meconium staining, 27
Medek, 20, 63, 74, 90, 119, 135–37, 193. See also CME therapy
Medicaid, 123–24
Micky D's, 132
microcephaly, 122
Moore, Beth, 56
MRI (magnetic resonance imaging), 15, 45, 57, 69, 89
myopia, 162

N

NACD, 71
NDT (neurodevelopmental treatment), 135, 139–40
New York City Board of Education, 129
NG tube (nasogastric), 28, 44, 88, 122
NICU (Neo Intensive Care Unit), 9, 28, 43, 76, 85–87, 89, 121–24
NJRSA (New Jersey Rett Syndrome Association), 77, 80
Novogroder, Azriel, 136–37
nystagmus, 69–70

O

Ontario March of Dimes, 129
OT (occupational therapy), 18, 28, 57, 59–60, 70, 78, 119–20, 123, 130, 168, 174
oxygen, 160

P

Parent's Guide to Special Education, A, 177
Pavlov, Ivan, 151

PDD (pervasive developmental disorder), 175
Pediasure, 45
Peto Institute, 128–30
PG Chambers School for Special Needs, 33
Piaget, Jean, 120
posturing, 17, 57, 83
Prevacid, 30
PRS (Pierre Robin syndrome), 42–43
PT (physical therapy), 18–19, 48, 57, 59–61, 63, 70, 74, 78, 90, 119, 123, 135, 138–40, 174
PVL (periventricular leukomalacia), 28, 89, 122, 124

R

reflux. See GERD (gastroesophageal reflux disease)
Reiki, 74
Rett, Andreas, 81
Rett syndrome, 76–77, 80–82
stages of, 82–83
Rett Syndrome Awareness Day, 80
Rice Dream, 60
Rifton Gait Trainer, 61
rigidity, 83
Robert Wood Johnson UMDNJ Medical School, 80
RSV (respiratory syncytial virus), 45
Russell, Alexander, 129

S

Santosh***, 66–69, 71–72, 74, 136, 152
scoliosis, 83
Seattle Children's Hospital, 43, 45

seizure, 46, 72, 81–83, 163
sensory therapy, 119
Skinner, B. F., 151
Social Security, 123–24
social worker, 14, 123–24
Somerset County Childhood
    Disability Resource Guide, 78
Somerset County Department of
    Human Services, 78
Somerset County Freeholders, 78
Somerset Patriots, 79
spasticity, 83
speech therapy, 18, 31, 60, 70, 74,
    119, 174
Spivack, Frida, 129–30
Steenblock (doctor)***, 169
stem cell therapy, 20, 50, 163, 166–
    69, 193
strabismus, 70
stroke, 27, 31, 45, 162–63
suit therapy, 135, 138–40, 168. See
    also TheraSuit

T

TD Bank Ballpark, 79
TEIS (Tennessee Early Intervention
    Services), 59–60
Thalheimer, Lori, 42, 157, 173, 193
Thalheimer, Madison, 49–50, 203
Thalheimer, Ryder, 42–50, 130, 136,
    157, 163, 193, 203
TheraSuit, 63, 119, 138–39. See also
    suit therapy
TheraTogs, 61–62
traumatic brain injury/disorder, 28,
    120, 124, 138–39, 154, 157, 162,
    166, 169, 201
Tsang, Vicky, 130

TTS (twin-to-twin transfusion), 26
Tunda (Ability Camp instructor), 130

U

UCLA, 151
United Cerebral Palsy, 129, 138
Universal Playground, 80
University of Wisconsin, 128

V

vision therapy, 119
VitalStim, 31, 61

W

wall walking, 46, 131
Wal-Mart, 132
Watson, John, 151
Williams syndrome, 89
Wyatt***, 85–92, 136

X

X-Cell Center, 167–69

Z

Zanaflex, 19

About the Authors

Author Tamara Lee Jacobson

As a special-needs mother with a background in education, I felt there was a huge void out there in the world of traumatic brain injuries and other genetic disorders.

I hold a dual degree in Theater Arts and Elementary Education with a minor in Political Science. My Masters is in English as a Second Language (ESL), with a concentration in Urban Education. I hold a post-graduate certificate degree in Administration and Supervision and Stage Direction. I taught Theater Arts, English as a Second Language, History, and Language Arts for over fourteen years and was a supervisor in a high school for three years. For seven years I owned my own theater arts studio in Warren, New Jersey. I was featured in 2011 Cambridge Who's Who in America, I will be a graduate of "Partners in Policy-Making 2012" with the Division of Developmental Disabilities Council in Trenton, New Jersey. Combining my interests in education and theater, I always included special-needs children in my theatrical productions. Therefore, when I was suddenly faced with my own special-needs child, I wanted to reach out to help those parents who don't understand how to ask for or receive services. It comes easy to me, but not to everyone. I want to help parents who have just found out that they, too, will be on a special journey with a special child. I wish that when I found out about my daughter's cerebral palsy, visual impairment, and apraxia, that I had someone laying out a solid roadmap for me.

At forty-one, I feel I am blessed. I have a need to give back to the community around me. I am truly lucky to have a child like Ella.

I have recently opened a business as a private special-needs advocate. I love the feeling of helping families learn about their rights, and I know I can help them achieve their positive goals for the future. I live in a wonderful suburb outside of New York City in Warren, New Jersey, with my supportive and helpful husband of twelve years Alan, and my three beautiful girls: Laura (age 8), my singing figure skater; Lexi, my dancing gymnast (age 6); and Ella, her funny and brave identical twin (age 6). We have a fantastic nanny, Sonia, who's been devoted to Ella for six years, and a sweetheart of a dog named Sami. I have the love and support of a great community and an amazing extended family, especially my mother, Dianne and father, Irwin.

Coauthor Lori Eichler

As a mother of a special-needs child, I have learned that in order to figure out what's important in life, pertaining to my child, I have to find the right information and learn from the right people. Since others can't always do this, I thought by writing a book about the exceptional people that I have met, and learning what's worked for them when caring for their special-needs child, I could help so many struggling parents out there who don't know what to do next. I'd love to be able to continue to act as a resource for families living on the West Coast.

I hold an Associate's Degree in Liberal Arts and played two years of fast-pitch softball and two years of basketball on a college scholarship. I was a postal carrier and clerk for ten years before I had Ryder, and then was fortunate enough to be able to quit my job in order to stay at home with him. I am an avid traveler. I've traveled around the United States and Canada exploring therapies with my son. Now I feel good about sharing with others. I'm convinced that you need to stay active in whatever it is that you are passionate about. Playing softball and hanging out with my great friends and family are a few of my special pleasures. I have an eighteen-year-old daughter, Madison, who I am very proud of.

I thank God for my family and friends because without them life would sometimes seem impossible.

Our

Life

Is

Good